SECRET AGENT
BRAINTEASERS

SECRET AGENT
BRAINTEASERS

SINCLAIR McKAY

Quercus

New York • London

New York • London

ISBN 978-1-63506-135-2

Library of Congress Control Number: 2019931705

Distributed in the United States and Canada by
Hachette Book Group
1290 Avenue of the Americas
New York, NY 10104

Manufactured in the United States

10 9 8 7 6 5 4 3 2 1

www.quercus.com

To top code-cracker Jean Valentine, a true inspiration. Ever since working for Bletchley Park, her enthusiasm for conundrums has never diminished and she likes to solve six impossible puzzles before breakfast. This is also for the ordinary men and women across the years who, when drawn into the realm of the secret services, have shown extraordinary bravery.

CONTENTS

INTRODUCTION

Of all idle childhood daydreams, it must surely be one of the most common: what is it like to be approached out of nowhere and invited to become a spy?

The fantasy might run something like this: a cryptic meeting, maybe amid the tall bookcases and red leather armchairs of a grand Pall Mall club; then the mission. A posting to a far-distant foreign city, pulsing with colour and rich fragrance. And a brief to blend in, to infiltrate sinister secret societies, with the aim of bamboozling your opponents to reveal classified information or forbidden documents. How far could you get without letting your nerves show?

And now the reality. By and large, the business of being recruited for the secret services is (relatively) transparent these days: no armchairs, no glasses of port. MI6 advertisements radiate friendly advice. But no matter how open and inclusive spooks might now wish to appear, the truly important things remain unspoken. The vetting is as daunting and unforgiving as it ever was; no friend of yours will go unchecked. And the essential clandestine requirements of the job stay hidden from view. These are broadly the same as they were over 100 years ago, when the official British secret services as we know them came into being. To be an agent, there are certain qualities one must possess.

Given how lethally serious and consequential the real work is, it is curious that when we think of spying, we still associate it with secrets whispered in shadowed corners, figures in black stealing through darkened rooms in search of classified documents, heavily accented femmes fatales, and agents receiving orders from brusque bosses behind walnut desks. In a touch-screen age of algorithms and GPS, this imagery ought to be antique. Funnily enough, though, it actually holds true in broad principle. This is because successful spying is all about human contact. These images also help explain the constant grip that espionage has over our imagination even today.

Now, it tends to be the case (as I have found) that those who have been employed by MI5 or MI6 enjoy making the point – with a faint smile – that actually the work is generally rather tedious, repetitive and colourless. This is a pose of immense worldliness, adopted by those who have clearly never known the tedium of much more ordinary workplaces.

And in a wider sense, it is quite simply untrue: regardless of the exact nature of the games that spies must play, the whole thing – even in the drabbest, greyest settings – inevitably crackles with the electricity of crucial geopolitical purpose.

Spying is an entire way of looking at the world. It is about observing people, landscapes, texts, and seeing concealed meanings. It is about interpreting language, searching for disguised significance. The spy does not have to be a great intellectual. What she or he does have to be is needle-sharp at understanding human nature.

And no matter how many technical leaps there have been in terms of ubiquitous electronic surveillance – whether hacking computers, phones or cameras – there still remains the fundamental spying divide: and it is defined by the terms 'sigint' and 'humint'. 'Sigint' is short for 'signals intelligence' – that is, the art of listening in to all the coded communications of opposing nations, and unravelling their meanings. But there is still a vital need for 'humint', short for 'human intelligence' – that is, the agents out there in the field, making contacts, forging alliances of trust, cajoling, listening and, where necessary, finding physical means of getting hold of intelligence. This is still the heart-pounding side of spying.

It has also been one of the great constants throughout history: as long as there have been civilisations, there have been spies. From biblical times to the modern-day era, the secret agent must be both brave enough and skilful enough to move among the enemy without being detected. Discovery can mean death. The ability to adopt new guises and personas can become a lethal version of a child's dressing-up game. In the earliest days of MI6 (the foreign-facing branch of the British secret service), at the start of the twentieth century, there was a fascination for and delight in disguises. One agent called Paul Dukes, infiltrating himself into revolutionary Russia, used an extraordinary array of wigs, false moustaches and different costumes in order to fraternise with murderous Bolsheviks and psychotic Cossacks.

Also there right from the start of MI6 was an open love for the latest technology and trick gadgetry. There was a general obsession with perfecting the ideal invisible ink, using materials that any agent might easily obtain, however unpleasant. One such – said to be quite successful – was semen.

There is something about the real-life looking-glass world of spying that the most popular fiction never quite seems to catch. In the case of Ian Fleming's James Bond, once you subtract the implausibly exotic women and the fairy-tale ogre villains, you are actually left with very little in the way of good honest espionage. Conversely, the weary operatives who populate John Le Carré's 'Circus', endlessly alert to traitors and moles, and ground down by the whole sour existential crisis of the Cold War, seem to see it all as a repellent charade.

For the rest of us, that is not how the daydream goes. There is that subconscious conviction that the whole business of spying must be both hugely exciting and also rewardingly virtuous. Not to mention elegant and sophisticated.

Perhaps one of the finest screen interpretations of the spying game as escapist fantasy is given in Hitchcock's *North by Northwest* (1959), in which advertising executive Cary Grant is mistaken for an agent in a smart New York club, subsequently finds himself chased down by assassins across the country and, as the escapade unfolds, actually evolves into the spy everyone has wrongly assumed him to be. The various ordeals – including being machine-gunned from a crop duster plane, and dangling off the edge of Mount Rushmore – appear to regenerate him. The moral of the story is that even if one is quite without morals, a spirit of adventure can still bring fulfilment.

Yet it is only comparatively recently that spies became folk heroes. Before the twentieth century, they were more often figures who inhabited a darkened world of shifting loyalties and multiple betrayals. In the febrile Elizabethan age, spying was very often a lethal business, a maze of torture and sudden violence. Paranoia about Catholic agents seeking to undermine Elizabeth's rule meant young men were sent to travel across the continent to gather intelligence about communication networks linking enemy countries such as Spain with contacts back in London: spies to root out spies.

Later, as the shockwaves of the French Revolution reverberated across the Channel, agents were sent deep undercover to Paris to try to evaluate any possible threat or risk of contagion to Britain. In those paranoid times, the Duke of Portland, heading up what was an early incarnation of a national secret service, was said to have recruited the young Romantic poet William Wordsworth, who travelled extensively throughout France and the various principalities of Germany.

And of course, spies have come over to Britain too: in the late nineteenth century, London's sawdust-strewn pubs jostled with young new arrivals from France, from Germany, from Russia. Some were revolutionary anarchists – mingling and plotting in pub back-rooms – but others had a more singular purpose: they were double agents from the Russian secret police seeking to eliminate political enemies. Some things change little across the years. Novelists and playwrights were starting to be drawn to this netherworld of codenames, secret signs, bombs and tumult. A popular literary serial at the time was 'Ruth the Betrayer', featuring all manner of underground cabals, hermetic passwords and pistol shots.

Women were central to these and subsequent blood-and-thunder narratives, but mainly as dark-eyed amoral enemy agents, ruthless about drawing ambassadors under their spells of enchantment, the better to creep into embassy studies in the dead of night to open official safes. As if answering some public demand for a real-life equivalent, there was, during the First World War, the tragi-comic distraction of the adventures of 'Mata Hari', whose assumed name was to find a form of immortality as the real woman behind it was gradually forgotten. As we shall see later, her real-life espionage exploits were almost designed for readers desperate for escapism. That stereotype continued long after the war in the works of Ian Fleming: Pussy Galore indeed! In the real corridors of the secret service, pioneering female agents of the 1960s such as Daphne Park faced a struggle to be taken seriously as equals. Dame Stella Rimington, who rose to head MI5 a couple of decades later, broke through that glass ceiling with aplomb.

Despite its limitations, fiction has sometimes been a surprisingly clear window into the reality of spying. It was at the end of Queen Victoria's reign that espionage in the service of empire first found its more certain expression in terms of public consumption: Rudyard Kipling's classic novel *Kim*, published in 1901, is both storming adventure and philosophical proposition. Set in India, this is a realm in which the young protagonist is eventually recruited to help the British secret services, and finds himself in the Himalayas facing Russian agents, and all while his elderly Tibetan lama companion is attempting to find enlightenment.

Here is where we also acknowledge the other huge draw of the world of espionage: that of the sinister enemies. In many cases, fiction writers have hardly had to exaggerate. Since Tsarist times, Russia appears to have specialised in giving the world undercover agents of unparalleled malevolence: from the Leninist agents of the Cheka, to the heavies of Stalin's NKVD, to the flinty and merciless assassins of the post-war KGB. It is almost as if the Russian intelligence services revel in their reputation for darkness. They have not been alone in this. In his 1966 novel *The Comedians*, Graham Greene creepily evoked the Tonton Macoute, the Haitian secret police of 'Papa Doc' Duvalier – but no fiction could be more chilling than the hideous reality.

The sense of an implacable foe is central. When we daydream of being recruited, we are holding in our heads the idea not merely of being sent on missions for Queen and country, but also squaring up to frightening and powerful enemies, who can only be thwarted with guile and wit. It is certainly the case that the secret services prize gazelle-like mental agility, the ability to extemporise, to think on your feet in an emergency. Who among us would have the level-headedness displayed by the aforementioned MI6 operative Daphne Park in an ambush deep in Africa in the early 1960s? With her jeep surrounded by gunmen not interested in hearing cover stories, she leaned over to the back seat, opened a wooden crate, reached inside and pulled out a bottle of whiskey with a broad smile. The other bottles in the crate were offered around and her smile proved contagious.

But there is another branch of fascination here too, and that is the psychology of those who betray their own side. The story of the Cambridge Spies – their recruitment at university in the 1930s, their rise within the secret services, the volume of material they passed to Stalin's Russia, and their subsequent unmasking – still inspire films, plays, novels and histories. Not because they were in any way anti-heroes but rather because they played such a hazardous game without ever losing poise. How did they not buckle?

In contrast to this moral murk, however, is the undeniably brighter side of espionage: the delight in the sheer inventiveness and occasional absurdity of the gadgets devised for use in the field. Who could ever decline a visit to Q's laboratory? This aspect of Bond's life was curiously accurate: MI6 really did have a Quartermaster (Q) and during the war and afterwards, there really were workshops devoted to adapting briefcases to contain daggers and gold coins, to disguising bombs as items such as potatoes, and to using sheep with fake fleeces as means of getting sensitive documents across borders.

The key word in all of this is 'intelligence': the justification for underhand methods, disguises, even betrayals. The agent will weave any deception necessary in order either to safeguard secrets, or to steal them. There is another term too: 'tradecraft' – an innocent word that seems to place the ability to break into forbidden zones and listen in on the enemy on the same level as carpentry or breadmaking. In the 1980s, *Spycatcher* author Peter Wright described with some relish how he and his colleagues 'bugged and burgled' their way across London. On one ethical level, this might make highly virtuous readers wince. But heavens, even the stiffest moral compasses can wobble a little when the cause is just, when it saves lives and – crucially – when it is just so juicy to read about.

So the puzzles here are designed to challenge you on a variety of levels. The question 'have you got what it takes?' does not refer to mere dexterity with words and numbers. They are also about how quickly you can summon your wits under pressure; how keen an eye you have for anomalies; how alert you are to tone when it comes to identifying friend or foe; how steely your logic is when required to find an escape route; how inspired and imaginative your lateral thinking is when confronted with poetic riddles in which the secrets are concealed.

Espionage is an ever-evolving contest: wits matched against counter-wits. Some of the puzzles here are historical conundrums of the sort that Edwardian and later agents would have been expected to tackle with speed. Some have been inspired directly by more modern secret service recruitment tests. Others, involving everything from radio transmission challenges to maps, are there to give you an idea of the practical proficiency needed out in the field.

Paradoxically, in an ever-changing, ever-unstable world, the spy will remain a constant. Because ultimately you will always need people who can divine the true intentions of others. Espionage might frequently be a dirty business – but in a more high-minded sense, it is also a branch of philosophy. Hopefully, this wide range of puzzles will also prove as beguiling, diverting and dazzlingly devious as any of the best secret agents!

CHAPTER ONE

THE TAP ON
THE SHOULDER

Perhaps I should begin with a confession. Back in my university days, there were rumours that a certain academic – a convivial figure who was popular with the students – was also a spy. He was said to work for one of the services; it was broadly assumed to be MI6.

Obviously, if he were to turn up in the same pub as some of his students in the evening, then none of this was ever mentioned. This was at a time (and this dates me) when the secret service acronyms MI5 and MI6 were rarely mentioned in the press or on television. They had no officially avowed existence. But all of this gave the academic an intriguing new dimension. The rumours alone made everyone look at him in a different way: here was a man who might be privy to all sorts of state secrets. More than that, it was rumoured that he was a recruiter. If you were felt to be a suitable candidate to be a spy, then the tap on the shoulder might well be coming from this man.

Later on in university, I got it into my head that I would probably make a rather brilliant spy. The notion, like so many others at the time, would have been as fleeting as a spring rain shower. But one evening, I happened to get slightly drunk in that pub and the academic was there so I decided to push matters on a little.

I marched up to him through knots of other students and had the following exchange. To his credit, he wore an expression of polite bemusement throughout.

'Can I be a spy?' I said.

'No,' he said.

So that was the end of my espionage career.

The puzzles in this section are designed to be rather more affirmative. Above many other qualities, recruiters at the security services have always looked out for those who have nimble problem-solving abilities: those who can speedily and effectively tackle common-sense and practical conundrums against a tight deadline.

Today, entrance into the world of espionage is properly schematised, with candidates being assessed closely and fairly. However, not all that long ago, recruitment tended towards the informal. Former MI6 officer Harry Ferguson recalled that in the early 1980s, as he was trying to decide on whether to take a career in the army, his university tutor asked him one day if he would like to work for his country.

Ferguson said that at that stage, he was not even particularly aware of the difference between MI5 (domestic counter-espionage) and MI6 (international operations). Yet out of curiosity he took the train to London and from that point became ever more closely pulled in, eventually joining the ranks of the MI6. He was being sounded out for the position of an officer, to be based in their headquarters rather than abroad. This is a distinction to be drawn all the way through the story of SIS (Secret Intelligence Services): the officers in London tend not to see action out in the field because they do not have the necessary cover to be able to move unobtrusively through other countries. For this, it is better to call upon people who can and these field agents have often been in business, or in journalism, or have been writers.

The secret service as we know it was formed in 1909; before then, the business of espionage was juggled between the War Office and the Foreign Office, spreading over various diplomatic missions and consuls. And before 1909, there were many figures who viewed the very idea of espionage and agents with the most profound distaste. How could such low-down deceptions and stratagems ever be carried out by gentlemen? And how could a gentleman assent to being recruited into such a trade?

Such dainty fastidiousness was offset by the understandable paranoia caused by the tense geopolitics of the early twentieth century, which was whipped up further by the ominous plotlines of popular fiction. It is sometimes asserted that the SIS was pulled together as a response to public hysteria caused by the spy stories of William Le Queux. Le Queux, a novelist who sold in his millions, imparted yarns of sinister German plots to invade Britain, using undercover operatives as spearheads. Newspapers wanted to know: was Britain ready for such a threat in real life?

But actually, the department assembled in 1909 was also chiefly a means of more effectively organising the spies that had already been operating on behalf of Britain for some time. There had always been secret agents. And sometimes, back then, the recruitment process had, out of necessity, been carried out very deep in the shadows.

Possibly the most famous instance came at the beginning of the twentieth century. The agent's real name was Shlomo Rosenblum. He had been born deep in the steppes of eastern Europe (the region that is now Ukraine) and even before he arrived in London in the late 1890s, there were a variety of wild tales attached to his name, including one involving him having worked for a British expedition in Brazil that got attacked by local villagers, which he apparently single-handedly saved. Later he was to call himself the name by which he is now remembered: Sidney Reilly.

Reilly went on to find terrific fame as one of the archenemies of the nascent Soviet Union and indeed as a possible womanising inspiration for 007; but he was attractive as a proposition to the late Victorian War Office department both because he had international business interests (he ran a company called Ozone Preparations) and because he had exceptional linguistic skills, being fluent in Russian, German, Polish and French.

Reilly's recruitment and early adventures seemed to set a sort of template. As a businessman, this sleek operator could set himself up anywhere in the world. He had a short spell in China at the turn of the century, where he was rumoured also to be spying for the Japanese, and he moved to Russia in 1906, when it was twilight in St Petersburg for the Tsarist era. Reilly's 'business' brought him into contact with a wide range of figures, both establishment and revolutionary. His ease with the language meant that he had no difficulty fitting in; and indeed he appeared to have no overt concerns about standing out, having decided to live in an apartment of notable opulence.

And so, as the new SIS was brought together several years later, it would have already been aware of the activities of this extraordinarily energetic figure and also of the need to draw him into the fold of this new bureau. Indeed, Reilly was also lured into working for the domestic side of this service, the department that would later become known as MI5.

After the First World War, in which military officers were drawn naturally into intelligence operations, the recruitment pattern started to settle into one that was distinctively civilian. One of the reasons we can all now fantasise about being pulled into this world is that from very early on, the secret services were drawing men and women in from all walks of life.

It is important to mention women at this point because during the years of the First World War, MI6 and the Belgians scored an extraordinary espionage victory over the Germans. A network of spies had been established by a Flemish telephone engineer called Walthère Dewé. The cover-name was La Dame Blanche – The White Lady. (The network was named after an old legend that proclaimed that the Hohenzolleren dynasty would be brought down by such an enigmatic lady.)

Having set up a base in Rotterdam, MI6 took to handling this ever-spreading web of intelligence, monitoring German activity everywhere. A large proportion of these willing recruits were women: watching troops, trains, tanks; clocking movements; overhearing orders and conversations. They were observing every move the German army made, down to the swish of a cavalry horse's tail.

Some of the methods used to ensure this intelligence got back safely anticipated some of Q's more outlandish schemes. Cakes of soap were adapted to carry messages, as were bars of chocolate.

Sometimes, a signal would be sent by means of a woman simply laying out some beans on a table or a window sill; each bean signifying some numbers or aspect of the German forces' movements. Longer messages were furled up and tucked into the hollow tubes of specially adapted broomsticks.

It was in the 1920s and 1930s that the secret services learned to spread the recruitment net wider. But the results could sometimes be dizzying. One of the more fascinating figures to be drawn into this world was Charles Maxwell Knight, known simply as 'Maxwell' or even more simply as 'M'. A former army officer and jazz band leader with a mania for animals that led to him turning his Sloane Square flat into a menagerie for small exotic birds and mammals, Knight came in to the orbit of MI5 via a meeting in a smart club with a businessman called Sir George Magkill.

In the 1920s, Knight's mission was to infiltrate a cell of British fascists; indeed, he did so with such uncanny success that he actually became that organisation's director of communications.

And it was from this position – in turn – that Knight recruited six young fascist men and set them with their own mission: to infiltrate an opposing communist cell. This they did. The communists were regarded in the mid-1920s as the graver threat; the British fascists, though foaming and racist, were not quite yet at the sleek Mosley-ite stage of black shirts and marches. What the story illuminates though, aside from the increasingly febrile state of interwar politics, is that particularly troubling aspect of spying: if one joins a fascist organisation, and helps to run it successfully, and blends in with the other fascists so effectively that there is not a particle of suspicion – then does that not suggest a sympathy with the cause that goes beyond acting?

But as Knight rose within MI5, his anti-Nazi instincts came more sharply into focus. This, added to his unceasing anti-communist fervour, gave him a rare energy. And if, by contrast, recruitment to sister department MI6 tended towards the bond of the old school tie – young men who had attended the smartest schools and Oxbridge and who came from what were then termed 'good families' – Knight was much more creative. He actively sought out men and women from a variety of backgrounds. Knight would go on to recruit some remarkable operatives, the most notable of whom were women.

Twenty-five-year-old Olga Gray was a typist from Birmingham who was sounded out at a garden party in 1931. Initially, it was her secretarial skills that made her such an outstandingly shrewd catch. Her brief was to infiltrate the British Communist Party, and to establish proof of its undercover links with Moscow. Olga, with her distinctive peroxide blonde hair, first started mingling at events for the Friends of the Soviet Union Society in London and then she was offered office jobs with the communists. She was so effective at her work that she soon became indispensable to them. As she rose ever higher through the hard-left hierarchy, she eventually worked for the leading figures Percy Glading and Harry Pollitt.

From the start, the intelligence that Olga Gray was bravely relaying to Maxwell Knight, from financial transactions to future plans, was extraordinarily good. At one point, though, the duality of her life brought her close to a nervous breakdown. In the mid 1930s, she withdrew only to have Glading and Pollitt beg her to return to the communist fold. They actually wanted to turn her into a Soviet agent.

She was sent on an ocean voyage to India to pass intelligence on to a Soviet agent in Mumbai; back in London, she was asked by the communists to establish a 'safe house' for members of the Party and their Russian guests. It was while she was living at this address that Olga Gray was approached by the communists to infiltrate the military arsenal at Woolwich, a vast establishment on the Thames in south-east London. Her brief was to obtain plans for weapons in development and pass them to Soviet Russia. All of this she duly relayed to MI5; and, taking care to conceal Olga's betrayal, her superiors moved in to arrest the ringleaders.

Another invaluable attribute that Olga Gray had was her extraordinary memory. She had perfect recall for the tiniest details. As the secret services developed further, this was one of the talents that recruiters would be specifically looking out for. Intellectual attainment was all very fine in its place, but the very practical skill of memorising faces and documents alike was more highly prized.

All this said, recruitment in the interwar and postwar years still tended – by default – to favour the more privileged social circles. In terms of being an officer, what apparently could not be shaken was this conviction that the most trustworthy people came from the smartest families. Sometimes the hiring occurred within families: in her recent captivatingly funny memoirs, novelist Charlotte Bingham recalled her own initiation in her section.

She landed a secretarial role in MI5 in the 1960s because her father, John Bingham, was a senior officer there and he felt it was time she had a job. John Bingham was said to have been the inspiration for John Le Carré's George Smiley. His daughter wrote of how he kept a revolver at home and carried a sword-stick; and sometimes went out on 'burglary' missions, involving breaking into suspect's houses. Yet in contrast to this, office life in MI5 seemed more like a girl's boarding school. Charlotte Bingham's female administrative boss was known as 'the dragon', and young women with names like Arabella would seek to exploit the dragon's known fear of spiders and her equal hatred of garlic and Roman Catholics.

In a broader sense, even the most direct nepotism might have been defended thus at the time: that given the need above all else for complete secrecy, it would hardly do to have such positions openly advertised to one and all. In official terms, and for wider public consumption, there was no such thing as a secret service. Everyone knew it was there; yet everyone was expected to elegantly pretend that it wasn't.

For a time in the post-war years, MI5 occupied a large and functionally ugly block in Curzon Street, Mayfair. Rather taking the edge off the intense confidentiality were the satirical bus conductors who, as their vehicles stopped on Park Lane, bellowed to all their passengers: 'Curzon Street and MI5!'

MI5 recruiter Maxwell Knight might have seen the funny side. As he saw it, a sense of humour was a terrifically important attribute to look for in potential spies. The ability to be funny, or to laugh at the wit of others, was an indicator of the general speed at which a person could think on their feet. Later recruiting officers also placed enormous importance on this for several reasons, not just because of mental agility, but also because laughing at daft things is quite the most brilliant way of relieving stress and making sure one keeps a sense of perspective.

So the puzzles in this section – while not perhaps testing the sensitivity of your funny bone – are exactly about quick-fire mental gymnastics. The ability to block everything else out in order to swiftly focus on a problem would be a valuable attribute for any candidate to the secret service.

1

A FIRST ASSIGNMENT

This is your first assignment. It is absolutely vital you follow the instructions carefully. Read everything on this page before you begin. If you fail in this, the mission will have to be aborted and your espionage career may be over before it has begun.

a) On Mondays, dad Simon and son Sam, along with baby Shaun, visit a local library to borrow sci fi books which Sam finds fascinating, Isaac Asimov particularly. Simon also borrows CDs as music is his passion, including Vaughan Williams, Mozart and Tchaikovsky. In addition, Simon plays horn and tuba in a band.

Cousins Susan and Sally both work in this building as librarians on Thursdays, Fridays and Saturdays, working hard to assist all who find it difficult to pick anything, from a hardback book to a monthly journal. On finishing work, Susan walks, but Sally is a train and bus fan, changing always at Park Road Station. Admit it, all this sounds a bit odd but can you say why?

b) Viv is a good mimic.
Dill is one of the ingredients in the mix.
Di can't find the pan lid.
Civil disobedience and disorder make me livid.
Lilli is frankly a bit dim.

There is a very specific link between all the above five sentences. What is it?

c) Having read all this, take no further action.

2

BUILDING BLOCKS

Offices, safe houses, apartment blocks, stately homes; all these and more have played their part in the world of espionage from its early days. In this puzzle, the letters in the names of buildings or parts of buildings have been mixed up and rearranged alphabetically. The names themselves are in no particular order. Solve the anagrams and place the answers horizontally in the grid so that the letters in the squares reading diagonally from top left to bottom right reveal a famous building.

E E E L P S T

A I M N N O S

C E H I M N Y

A A C H R W Y

E E H K L O Y

B D I O O R U

E E L M P S T

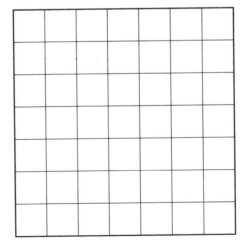

3

DIARY DATE

Everyone needs a break, and occasionally in the early years of MI5 and MI6 the stresses and strains of this way of life proved almost too much for some to bear. You are planning ahead for next year when you take a much-needed holiday. The following list has been sent to you so that you can fill a key date in your diary. When will that holiday be?

A D _ _ _ C T

C _ _ _ I C I O U S

D I S _ _ _ E D

D _ _ _ O R A T E

G _ _ _ E D

I N _ _ _ A T I V E

I N _ _ _ I S I V E

L I _ _ _ O A T

R E _ _ _ K A B L E

T R A N _ _ _ _

T R O _ _ _ S

4

FOR SAFE KEEPING

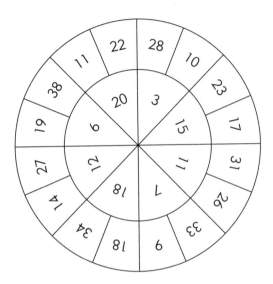

You have succeeded in getting to the strong room but your final hurdle is the safe itself. There is a ring of numbers on the outside of the combination lock and a ring of numbers on the inside. Are they linked? Are they not linked? You know that the combination is made up of three different numbers.

Can you crack the code and open the safe?

5

HYMN PRACTICE

Retired information gatherer, the Reverend Cheetham, has made sure the hymn numbers for the morning service are displayed on the hymn board as usual. There are going to be four hymns sung at the service but in order to stir the congregation out of its slumbers he has posed a challenge to them. 'Can you move just TWO single numbers,' he says, 'so that all three vertical columns add up to the same amount? You cannot have two identical numbers in any column.'

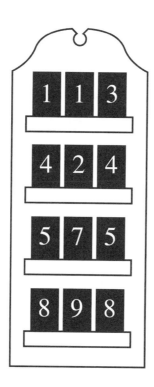

6

LINKS

Here you are tested on your ability to make connections between words. The words in Column 1 link to those in Column 3 by a middle word that joins the two. Can you find the missing links and reveal the message reading down in Column 2?

COLUMN 1	COLUMN 2	COLUMN 3
DOUBLE	_____	COURAGE
ESTATE	_____	ORANGE
FREE	_____	POWER
GREEN	_____	PAPER
NOW	_____	AFTER
PALM	_____	SCHOOL
PETROL	_____	OPENER
WITH	_____	ALL
SKELETON	_____	HOLE
HITHER	_____	WARDS
MORSE	_____	BREAKER

7

MISSING DELEGATIONS

Three countries are absent from an important meeting. Which countries are they?

First of all, complete the names of the food dishes below with the name of a nationality. Hunt these words out in the wordsearch letter grid. Nationalities may go across, backwards, up, down or diagonally but are always in a straight line. Draw a line through the letters you have used.

Now take the unused letters, reading left to right, top to bottom, and the countries whose delegates are absent will be revealed.

1	_____	CHOCOLATES
2	_____	COFFEE
3	_____	DELIGHT
4	_____	FRIES
5	_____	GOULASH

6	_____	MUSTARD
7	_____	OMELETTE
8	_____	PASTRY
9	_____	ROLL
10	_____	YOGURT

8

NEW RECRUIT

Olga Gray was recruited as an MI5 agent in 1931 when she was in her twenties.

In this puzzle you must use her name to discover a password. Make two 4 x 4 word squares from the list below where the words read the same across and down. The password is the word left over which will fit into neither square.

AURA	GRAY	PAGE
BAGS	MASK	POEM
EGGS	OLGA	SAYS

9

ON THE MOVE

You have been playing a waiting game, but now the call has come in that your section is being mobilised without delay. How are you getting to your four locations? The instructions below are all you have to go on!

1   _ _ _ H

    R O _ _ _ T

    R H O M _ _ _

    _ _ _ I N E S S

2   N I R _ _ _ A

    S A _ _ _ N A H

    _ _ _ I L L A

    A D _ _ _ T A G E

3   S _ _ _ I E S

    _ _ _ L E

    M A _ _ _ R E

    S _ _ _ B A R D

4   _ _ _ _ P

    B E R _ _ _ _

    _ _ _ _ M E L

    E X _ _ _ _ U R A L

10

SHADOWY SQUARE

Who knows which shadowy world you might enter after receiving that 'tap on the shoulder'!

Solve the quick-fire clues below. Write the five-letter answers vertically in the square. You must decide the order in which they go. When this is correctly completed, the letters in the first and third rows reading across will spell out a surveillance term, which you might have to negotiate!

OF THE COUNTRYSIDE

KENT PORT

FOE

MALE RELATIVE

HANGMAN'S ROPE

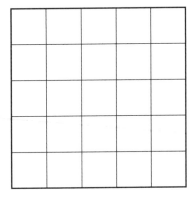

11

SPY RINGS

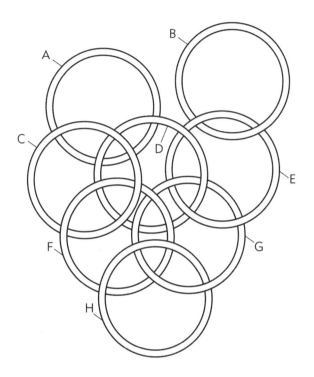

Infiltrating spy rings is all part of secret service skills. The Cambridge Spy Ring, which recruited agents in the 1930s, and the Portland Spy Ring, active in the 1950s, all have their place in history. Spy rings are all about connections.

Which of the rings A to H has the most links?

12

TOUR OF DUTY

Our diplomat is taking part in an international tour of duty which takes him all over the world. CHINA is his first posting and the first name on the list. Use the symbols to work out the names of the other countries where he is posted and say where the tour of duty ends.

13

VALUED AGENTS

All agents are of value to the people who employ them. A constant factor here is that all the agents are given a number, which links to their names.

IAN IS AGENT 6

NINA IS AGENT 9

TINA IS AGENT 10

ANITA IS AGENT 11

ANNE IS AGENT 12

Which agent number is given to ANNETTE?

14

WORKING IN PAIRS

The search is on for an English couple who are working together, and you have to find out their first names. You have been told that these names begin with adjacent letters of the alphabet.

Here's what you must do. Complete the words below. A pair of letters begins the word and the same pair completes it. When you have finished take the five pairs of letters you have used i.e. ten letters in all and use them to make the two first names which you are searching for.

1   _ _ C A P _ _

2   _ _ U C A T _ _

3   _ _ A S S U _ _

4   _ _ O N _ _

5   _ _ S U L _ _

CHAPTER TWO

THE SECRETS OF THE BUTTERFLIES

Winston Churchill had a small but daring spying adventure of his own in 1900. He was a reporter with the army in South Africa, posted there to chronicle the British war with the Boers. At one point, with the Boers in retreat from some territories, young Churchill was anxious to get his report, plus an interview with the military top brass, back to London, and he knew that he could do it from a British HQ on the other side of Johannesburg. He could either take a very long route around the Boer-occupied city or he could disguise himself and bluff his way through the centre.

He was advised that to ride across Johannesburg on horseback would be too conspicuous. So Churchill decided instead to ride a bicycle through the city. He found himself some suitably drab civilian clothes and a soft hat. In the catastrophic circumstances of the Boers stopping and detaining him, he was to speak French to maintain a pretence of having nothing to do with the British army.

Churchill got on his bicycle. As he rode through Johannesburg, he was piercingly aware that arrest would lead to a court-martial that would find that he was a spy. He recalled coming across a patrol of Boer soldiers and looking one of them directly in the eye. The soldiers moved off and so did Churchill. Once he had reached British HQ, he was ready to report his observations of Boer positions throughout the course of the journey. Even from a young age, Churchill had always regarded spying as the grandest game.

Despite the fact it was not the sort of thing that military officers had much enthusiasm for themselves, the geopolitical manoeuvres that were taking place across the world at the turn of the previous century, from the Sahara Desert to Tibet, meant that there always had to be some kind of system for intelligence gathering.

And so it is that the puzzles in this section will reflect that high Victorian sensibility, plus also a flavour of the slightly later spy fictions of John Buchan; for these had the most extraordinary influence on the real security departments that were to develop.

In the late Victorian age, there was room in the army for men who thought at a slightly different angle to their fellows. One such was Horatio Kitchener, the son of an Irish landowner widely detested by his tenants. Young Kitchener decided very early on that his future was in the army, and after receiving his commission, it was not long before he was being drawn into the sphere of intelligence gathering.

This was in the Sudan in the 1880s, a time when Islamist forces were in the ascendant. Kitchener proved adept both at disguise – he adopted Arab clothing – and linguistic expertise. And so it was that he would embark upon long missions taking him through searing desert and tiny villages, listening to all that was being said in these communities, weighing up strengths and weaknesses, never once being detected. That ability to absorb an entire language – Kitchener's Arabic was superb – was to become a chief intelligence requirement generally.

Alas, while the quality of the intelligence that he brought back was rich and detailed, it was not quite detailed enough. The troops sent into Sudan in 1883 were not prepared for the united thousands, well armed and trained, who rose up and rebelled; the result was a gory wipe-out of British forces. Kitchener, who would return to the region some years later in a position of military command, ensured that the lesson was absorbed.

Kitchener went on to find a form of immortality that in a curious way might have pleased him. His is the face with the piercing eyes staring out from that famous poster: 'Your Country Needs You!' Like many spies, he had secretly also craved some form of recognition and fame.

Elsewhere, British and Russian agents were engaged in lethally dangerous manoeuvres in the mountains of north-west India and

Afghanistan throughout the mid to late years of the nineteenth century. The Russians had been making substantial advances towards Britain's most prized colonial possessions and a bitter diplomatic confrontation ensued, remembered now as 'the Great Game'. Espionage in this case was carried out in some of the remoter, wilder regions. And sometimes, the spies concerned were (strictly speaking) amateurs.

One ruse was to use mapmakers for the purpose of intelligence gathering; the mountains of the Hindu Kush were still, in parts, unknown. But while the cartographers were comprehensively cataloguing topography, they were also carefully monitoring the movements of the small teams of Russians also to be found moving through the area. So the maps themselves could be used to convey intelligence on two levels: the straightforward lie of the land, and the disposition of the enemies advancing on it.

But there were other rather more perilous methods, sometimes used by young officers, and that was to assume disguises before heading into hostile territory. One cover frequently used was that of horse-dealer, but there were a few who even pretended to be mild-mannered clerics. Their missions required them to come to understandings with suspicious local inhabitants but there were frequently betrayals and misunderstandings. One unmasked British officer, operating deep in Afghanistan, was tortured and beheaded.

As well as encroachment from Russians, there were ferocious local conflicts to consider too. One of the more totemic figures of that time was a former soldier called George Hayward, who had resigned in order to become an explorer. With funding from the Royal Geographical Society in London, he was asked in 1869 to make a survey of the Pamir Mountains, deep in central Asia. Even though his own motivation was to explore a then unknown part of the world, the ensuing map would also clearly be an invaluable tool for military intelligence.

As his expedition went deeper into uncharted territory, so the hazards multiplied: he was imprisoned by mistrustful local authorities and was ill equipped to face some extraordinarily hostile mountain terrain. It was only by some miracle that he and his team did not freeze to death trying to move through snowdrifts that were almost shoulder-height. There were less obvious – but no less deadly – dangers too. Muslims and Hindus were at war in the region of Kashmir, and Hayward was publicly critical of Kashmir's Maharajah. This brought an explosion of anger from Britain; the Maharajah was seen as an ally.

A little time later, Hayward was working near Darkot, a tiny village high in the Hindu Kush. Intelligence reached him one day in July 1870 that unknown enemies were planning to murder him. It is said that he stayed up all that night and then fell into an uneasy sleep just before dawn. This was when the killers struck, first tying his hands behind his back. They then left his corpse in a perfunctory shallow grave, covered with a few pebbles. The body was later discovered by a Kashmiri soldier, and given a rather more dignified reburial in an orchard outside the village. Was Hayward a victim of the Maharajah or were there other agents who wanted to see him out of the way? The mystery was never quite resolved.

Elsewhere, there were those who regarded spying as a straightforward lark. One such was Robert Baden-Powell, a much-decorated soldier later to become famous for inaugurating the Boy Scout movement. There is much in Scout training that seems curiously to echo preparations for espionage. Even the basic game of hide and seek could be regarded as infant training for operating out in the field. Certainly Baden-Powell, this most imperial figure, was keen to stir an idea that espionage could be a noble, rather than ignoble, pursuit. He wanted to show that it wasn't all about sinister meetings and deceitful disguises. Quite the reverse – any boy should thrill to the gung-ho possibilities on offer.

Baden-Powell's own espionage experiences had ranged from monitoring German spies on British soil – one, a 'coal merchant' in Hull who had never been detected buying or selling a single lump – to undertaking reconnoitre missions in faraway lands. This was in addition to his military experiences, the most memorable of which was the Siege of Mafeking during the second Boer War. As this crisis ground on, Baden-Powell devised ruses to wrong-foot his Boer foes, who were monitoring his troops through binoculars; these included marking out faked minefields and getting soldiers to act out picking their way over barbed wire between trenches. There were no mines, no barbed wire, but Baden-Powell knew that Boer spies would be observing and reporting on these obstacles, and taking them into account in battle plans.

In the high Victorian age, spies were operating without the benefit of clever technology. The ingenuity was nonetheless admirable. Baden-Powell became an expert not only in coded hieroglyphs, but also in rather more unusual forms of information gathering.

He recalled how, in the Balkans, he had once posed as an eccentric butterfly collector; armed only with a sketchbook, he made his way out into the country and up into the hills. Any soldier or figure of authority he encountered, he would engage with a barrage of questions about local species of butterflies and moths. No one seemed keen to prolong these dialogues and he was largely left free to sit there with the sketchbook and his watercolours.

As a result no one noticed that Baden-Powell was secretly sketching the positions of field guns and the dimensions of fortresses. However, anyone stopping him and examining the book would instead see rather beautiful wildlife drawings. But how?

Baden-Powell himself explained the ruse in his memoirs, the brilliantly titled *My Adventures as a Spy*: 'They did not look sufficiently closely into the sketches of butterflies to notice that the delicately drawn veins of the wings were exact representations, in plan, of their own fort, and that the spots on the wings denoted the number and position of guns and their different calibres.'

Yet it occurred to many within Whitehall and Scotland Yard that if the British had such clever techniques, then foreign powers might also be equally cunning. It was at the dawn of the Edwardian era that a generalised paranoia about the presence of German agents operating within England began to intensify.

Spies were seemingly spotted everywhere. Suspicious and unfamiliar figures appeared to loiter near the great docks of Southampton; men were seen sitting on the heights of cliffs facing out to the grey sea and apparently sketching sea-forts. An isolated house on the Romney Marshes in Kent became the focus of speculation that it was being used as a base for a whole range of German agents; there were apparent sightings of furtive military training taking place out among those rustling reeds and glittering rivulets of the marsh, and reports that young men had been seen entering and leaving the house but never seemed to stay any length of time.

Yet as is sometimes remarked, even if some tales were far-fetched, it was nonetheless possible to be paranoid with good reason. In the years before the First World War, there were indeed a few opportunistic German spies in Britain, and they were focusing their efforts on getting information on the Navy and its latest weaponry. One spy, a doctor of philosophy called Max Schulz, went about his espionage using a technique that might charitably be termed double bluff: he had a houseboat in Portsmouth from which he flew the German flag, and he hosted parties for naval personnel at which he asked them perfectly openly about all the latest developments back at base. It was not too long before he was brought to trial.

Another German operative had a rather more enterprising idea: this was to acquire the lease of a public house in Rochester, Kent, near the mighty Chatham naval base. Thus all the intelligence would come directly to his bar; officers would be happily lubricated and talk would get looser as the evening went on. It took counter-intelligence officers longer to detect this extraordinary gambit: whoever in the world would suspect a jovial, flush-cheeked pub landlord of treachery?

And this is not to say that in that final gold sunset of peace before the onset of the Great War that British agents were not themselves fully active: there were men in Bremen and ports dotted along the North Sea trying to get intelligence on the secrets of the Kaiser's fleet. One agent was arrested in the teeth of a gale as he was attempting to sketch the details of German sea forts.

Yet the more of this was reported, the more it seemed that fact was only just beginning to catch up with the lurid fictions of the previously mentioned William Le Queux. He had terrific hits with novels such as *England's Peril* (1899) and *The Czar's Spy* (1905), which brought all the apparatus of the spy genre together, setting the tone for future generations of spies both real and unreal alike. His was a (relatively) fast-moving world of motor cars and telegrams, and in thrillers like *The Man from Downing Street* (1909), there were also chases involving trains. There was even, in a later adventure, a prototype green death ray.

Le Queux also gave readers some double-dealing scarlet women, moving within the smartest echelons of society. Chiefly, though, he solidified the popular notion of the enemy within, and it was as a result of his work that in real life, alert members of the public up and down the country were reporting imagined enemy espionage activity. One retired colonel deep in the Kentish countryside contacted the authorities after having witnessed, one dark night, some curiously flashing lights near the blackness of a railway tunnel. It seemed obvious to him that these were enemy agents signalling one another near the railway line, perhaps as part of some sabotage plot. In fact, it turned out to be campers.

Some of the protagonists of these exciting novels were men pulled into a vortex of plots and espionage almost, one might say, by happy chance – such as John Buchan's fictional hero Richard Hannay. And curiously, the newly formed British secret services, immediately prior to the slaughter of the war, seemed to approach their work in much the same spirit of intoxicating excitement. One newly recruited officer was told that spy work was 'capital sport'.

Even their German counterparts thought so too; in the immediate aftermath of one spying trial, where the German operative in question was found guilty and sentenced to four years in prison, there was, according to historian Christopher Andrew, an extraordinary scene in the court-room as the British agents went to shake the spy's hand.

The war was to change this, as it was to change all else. But the puzzles in this section retain some of that curiously innocent flavour.

1

BUTTERFLIES

Butterflies have patterns with two matching halves. In this puzzle you must find the matching halves of words, e.g butter and flies (although you might have gone down the wrong route and paired butter with cup!).

Look at the 23 short words below and pair them up to make eleven longer words. Clearly there is a short word left over. What other short word can you join to the end of this to make the twelfth longer word? We have given you a clue by strategically slotting in a question mark!

ACRE	HAT
ACTED	IMP
ANT	LAIN
ARM	LENT
ATE	LIPS
BAR	MASS
BUOY	OUR
CANDID	?
CATER	RACKS
CHAP	RAGE
COVE	RED
EXCEL	TICK

2

GIFT BOX

Seemingly innocent and highly decorated boxes are sent across the globe, containing exotic and wonderful gifts, or samples of rare and beautiful flowers or insects. However the boxes are often clever hiding places used to send highly secretive intelligence from overseas.

Here is a flat piece of card used to construct a six-sided box. Below are six examples of completed boxes. Only one matches the original piece of card. Can you work out which one it is?

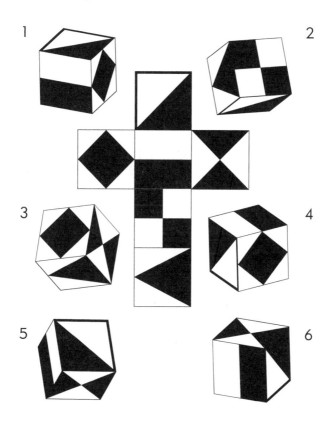

3

LEFT LUGGAGE

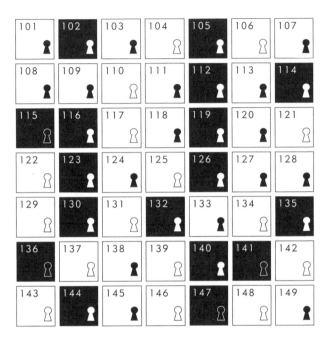

You arrive at a large railway station in the heart of the city on your grand tour around the world. You have received a mysterious instruction to pick up a parcel that has been left in a station locker. You know that the locker's number is more than 100 and less than 150, but you have not been given the exact number. You do have some scraps of information that can lead you to the correct locker.

- The locker's door and handle colour are not the same.
- The total of the three digits in the number is greater than five.
- It is directly above a locker with a white door.
- The locker with the next highest number has the same colour of door handle as your locker.

Which is the locker that you need to open?

4

SECRET SIGN

Throughout the 1870s to the 1890s, the comic operettas of Gilbert and Sullivan were the must-see events in London theatre. Famed for topsy-turvy flights of fantasy, Gilbert loved to poke fun at the figures of the day and topical trends. By the time of *The Grand Duke* – their last show together – the subject of spying came to feature. Gilbert's association of spies had a most eccentric way of giving a secret sign to others that they were part of the clandestine organisation: they had to eat a sausage roll!

Here's a less gluttonous, though equally strange way, of recognising fellow agents.

Someone appears and says to you, 'Ingot and chain. Kneed and fizzy. Ferns and . . .' He awaits your response. Assuming you are part of the secret group what do you say? A clue: it's nothing to do with sausage rolls.

5

PARLOUR GAME

Snakes and Ladders was a popular parlour game in the Victorian era. A similar game of Indian origin was called Moksha-Patamu. Both these board games had a moral dimension with ladders allowing you to move to a higher plane and snakes providing a journey in the opposite direction.

Fit the twenty-five words listed overleaf on to the Snakes and Ladders board starting with the letter V. Follow the direction of the arrows. The last letter of one word is the first letter of the next. When your word finishes at the foot of a ladder, repeat the letter at the top of the ladder and continue with the word chain. Similarly, when your word finishes at the head of a snake, repeat the letter at the other end of the snake and and proceed until the grid is complete.

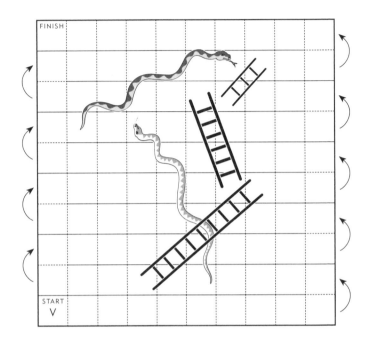

ALLOW	FRUIT	LIVER	SCARF	UNITE
COYPU	GREAT	MITRE	SHACK	VERDI
DRESS	HOTEL	OWING	TOTEM	WALTZ
EQUIP	IDIOT	PIANO	TOWED	YOUTH
ESSAY	KOALA	RELIC	TREES	ZEBRA

6

POINTED

You are handed the message below along with a compass. Where are you going? When?

_ _ D _ _ _ D A Y / _ V _ _ ! _ G /
_ _ V _ _ / F I F T _ _ _.

_ _ X T / _ _ _ K _ _ D / _ _ / _ _ _ D /
T O / M _ _ T / I _ /

T H _ / T _ _ T / _ _ A R / T H _ / B _ _ D /
I _ / T H _ / P A _ _.

_ I _ _ / T _ _ _ T Y.

7

ROAD BLOCK

Your mission takes you to the mountains of central Asia. Your cover is blown but in true gung ho spirit you are not going to give in without a fight. There are many roadblocks along your escape route. In order to create the maximum disruption you want to go through and smash as many roadblocks as you can. Exits can be made at any of the roads on the right.

Without retracing or crossing a route, what is the maximum number of blocks that can be encountered?

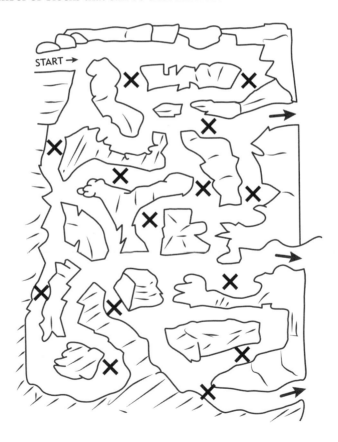

8

THE 39 STEPS

Step to it and start at step 0 and move through linked boxes to finally arrive at step 39. The total of the numbers that you pass on the way must total exactly 39. You can make as many moves as you like, but you cannot visit the same step twice. Award yourself the Richard Hannay gold award if you find the route at the first attempt.

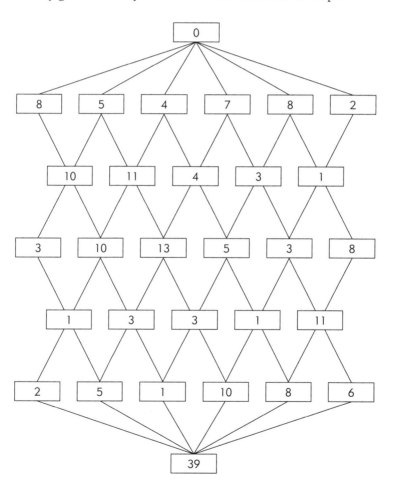

CHAPTER THREE

A MAN CALLED C

If there is one particular thread running through the story of British espionage that links today's touch-screen world with earlier days, it is that of a certain eccentric innovation. At the inception of MI6, for instance, in the long corridors of a gaunt Edwardian office block in St James's Park, there would be a noise like a recurrent whirring, accompanied by a distant, rhythmic thump. The noise drawing closer would herald the arrival, upon a child's scooter, of the first head of the British Secret Service.

In 1914, Sir Mansfield Cumming had lost a leg in horrific circumstances: a car crash in which his son was the driver. With his leg almost completely severed, Cumming crawled across the wreckage to reach his dying son. A later rumour had it that he was trapped by the leg, and that he had completed the amputation there and then with a pen-knife. Whatever the truth, the scooter was the enterprising means by which he moved through the offices of MI6.

It might reasonably be expected that the chief of a secret service should have a little of the night about him: a hint of darkness, the better to face Britain's ruthless opponents. Yet every account of Mansfield Cumming instead emphasises what seemed to have been an unquenchably effervescent spirit.

So the puzzles in this section will reflect this, together with some deviously delightful problems from an era when MI6's first agents were being pulled into the organisation – elegant but challenging logic tests, variations on brain-pummelling themes that they might well have seen in the classroom or university.

Certainly, Mansfield Cumming took pleasure both in deviousness and the unexpected. He always went by the simple designation

'C', which obviously inspired the 'M' figure of Ian Fleming's Bond novels. The 'C' simply stood for Cumming. He always wrote in green ink, which became a tradition for all subsequent heads of MI6 and continues to this day.

Yet for such a trailblazing figure in espionage, Mansfield Cumming actually had a remarkably un-spooklike background. Born in 1859, it seemed when he was young that his vocation would be the sea. He joined the navy, rose to become a sub-lieutenant, and had some adventures on his voyages: he was on a ship in the 1870s that was detailed to take on Malay pirates in the Indian Ocean. There was, however, one fatal obstacle standing in the way of Cumming's further progress: he suffered terribly from chronic seasickness. No amount of time spent at sea could acclimatise him. And so it was that at a relatively young age, he was forced to retire to dry land.

He spent some time as personal secretary to the Earl of Meath but was called upon to return to the naval base at Southampton to oversee a new experimental defensive measure at sea – the laying of nets, or 'booms'. This was what he was doing in 1909 when he was approached by an old naval colleague of his, Admiral Alexander Bethell, who had been asked among others in Whitehall to construct the infrastructure for a new more tightly organised secret service. Bethell contacted Cumming with the tantalising promise of 'something good'. Cumming was fifty, and he viewed the appointment as a welcome way of giving more service until, as he put it, he was 'shelved'.

Cumming's sometimes quirky good humour had uses other than raising morale; there were some who recalled how, when he was interviewing young potential recruits, he would take a pen-knife from his desk and suddenly, violently, thrust it into his leg. Those who flinched at the sight were deemed not suitable for spying duties (he had of course stabbed the wooden leg). The story might be taken with a pinch of salt – he would hardly be likely to turn away a possible recruit who had mastery of different languages and business contacts in every continent – but it is a nice suggestion of the psychological games that his department would engage in.

At the beginning of his new job, life was quiet, but come the First World War, Mansfield Cumming's department roared into life (the previously mentioned 'Dame Blanche' espionage operation being a particular success). And by the end of the war, it was quite clear to Cumming, and to Captain Vernon Kell, his opposite number in MI5, that the new enemy was communism.

In contrast to Cumming, MI5's Vernon Kell was almost over-qualified for his role as a spy chief; aside from his military career, he had also travelled extensively with his wife Constance, and was dazzlingly fluent in seven different languages, among which were Russian and Cantonese. He was a more retiring figure, and a little later in his career, Kell's colleagues could not quite fathom why his chauffeur-driven car flew a tiny flag or pennant with an image of a tortoise on it.

Before the war, he had had some serious success rounding up the most devious and dangerous of the German spies, who had been reporting directly back to an espionage chief called Steinhauer. After the war, the focus was very much on the Soviet Union, and the men and women in Britain who had been inspired by the Bolshevik cause. The aim was to fight subversion.

But MI5's perceived antagonism towards socialism created an initially awkward relationship with Ramsay MacDonald, elected Britain's first Labour Prime Minister in 1924. Then (rather like now), Labour was suspicious of the secret services. MacDonald himself wondered why Kell and MI5 devoted so much of their time to politicians and activists on the left when they might also be monitoring figures on the far right. There was a sense from MacDonald that he regarded their work as slanted and biased against Labour generally. The publication in late 1924 of the fake Zinoviev letter – purporting to be from a Russian to a British communist cell, encouraging subversion and a general uprising – continues to cast a shadow today. As it happened, though, just because that particular letter was a hoax did not mean that there wasn't any such communication. In fact, as later years were to prove, links between Russia and various British communists and trade unionists were extremely active.

Back at MI6, it was all change. Sir Mansfield Cumming died in 1923. But the new 'C', Admiral Sir Hugh Sinclair, was as exuberant as his predecessor. Sinclair's nickname was 'Quex', drawn from a nineteenth-century play by Sir Arthur Pinero called *The Gay Lord Quex*, a character who was the 'wickedest man in London'. The Admiral never wore naval uniform. And his colleagues were puzzled by his affectation of a bowler hat which seemed a little too small for his head, and which he jammed on with some force.

Unlike the more retiring Vernon Kell, Quex had a taste for the most lavish form of sociability; visitors to his office would be offered cigars from a crocodile-skin case. And business discussions would be conducted over exquisite meals at the Savoy. Hugh Sinclair was very popular with senior Whitehall figures, and had their fullest confidence. In a curious way, this is in itself one of the methods by which intelligence might be said to succeed; for when information is drawn from the shadows, and is not always recorded in signed documentation, the appearance of confidence in that information is essential for convincing others of the truth of it.

There are further curious little historical parallels to be drawn with those inter-war years and the apparent diplomatic situation today, one of which is Soviet Russia's reactions of petulant hurt whenever proof of espionage was uncovered. Another similarity is each side's interest in the other's technological know-how. The late 1920s brought Soviet trade missions to London; espionage is not just about assessing your opponents' military capabilities, but also finding out about leaps in industrial technology. These trade missions were monitored assiduously by a network of special constables who had been recruited specifically for such work.

Incidentally, today's equivalent of spies jostling around in 'trade missions' is the five-star world of the international conference. As scientific experts and businessmen and politicians gather in luxury hotel resorts from Dubai to Shanghai for conferences, so secret agents from a variety of nations move among them, ostensibly as delegates, seeking specialised knowledge, set on striking clandestine deals.

Back in the 1920s, Quex Sinclair also had responsibility for the Government Code and Cypher School, a department of outwardly certifiable cypher geniuses, who shared his intense distaste for communism. By the 1930s, it was also becoming grimly apparent that there were even more pressing threats materialising in Germany, Italy and Japan. The difficulty for Quex and MI6, as well as for many ministers in the 1930s, was not trying to decide if Hitler was horribly dangerous or not – he very obviously was – but how precisely to deal with him.

Some years later, the historian (and former wartime intelligence officer) Hugh Trevor-Roper was scathing about MI6 under Quex. He wrote of how the recruits tended to split into two types: public school men more acquainted with the grand gentlemen's clubs than anything approaching the real world, and former officers from the Indian police, not noted for any sort of intellectual curiosity. Trevor-Roper asserted that none of them will have read *Mein Kampf* nor indeed, conversely, have gone anywhere near the works of Marx. In other words, the secret services were composed of Bertie Wooster-style hapless posh boys and knuckle-headed colonials.

But this is not fair; there were some seriously intelligent figures being fostered within the services, learning all the skill required in infiltration, making trusting contacts, and maintaining secret relationships with those contacts knowing that any discovery could lead to reprisals and death.

In MI6, there was an officer called Frank Foley. No dissolute aristocrat, he had been educated by Jesuits, and had been recruited to be a 'passport control officer' in Berlin. This job description was the standard covering gambit for British spies at the time. Foley, who had perfect German, was assiduous at building contacts and relationships at a time when the skies above Germany were fast darkening. He saw exactly what the ascendancy of Hitler would mean, and most particularly, he understood the hideous danger to the Jews.

Foley is now remembered as the British Schindler. As Nazi Germany went to war, and its murderous intentions towards the Jews became daily clearer, Foley – who had no diplomatic immunity

– arranged means of escape through his work as a passport officer. Under Nazi rules, visas to Palestine became viciously, mockingly expensive: the then enormous sum of £1,000 was being asked of people who had had all their assets seized by the Nazis. Foley quietly charged £10 on the 'understanding' that the remainder would be paid upon arrival in Palestine. No such remainders, of course, were ever demanded or expected.

In 1939, Foley entered a concentration camp personally, with visas that he said had been delayed, but which by rights belonged to some of the prisoners. These prisoners – much to their astonishment – were taken into an office to see a mild, bespectacled man whom they had never met before about to open the gates to freedom and survival. It is reckoned that Frank Foley saved the lives of some ten thousand Jews.

It is true that back in London, Quex did not seem so alive or sensitive to the evil that was being done; indeed, he fretted about the numbers of Jewish refugees coming to England. And in the late 1930s, it also seemed that he was as much in favour of appeasement as Prime Minister Neville Chamberlain. He could not frame any other response to Hitler's seizure of the Sudetenland and then Czechoslovakia.

Conversely, Vernon Kell (or 'K') at MI5 had never been in any doubt about what the Nazis would be capable of doing if left unchallenged. Indeed, MI5 had been issuing warnings to Whitehall for several years about everything from rumoured plans of attack to Hitler's attitude towards Britain. Kell had had the foresight to recruit an invaluable source: a German aristocrat called Wolfgang zu Putlitz who had been working at the embassy in London for some years. Putlitz had witnessed the rise of the Nazis and seen how the embassy had now become home to SS agents. Putlitz was gay and his partner Willy Schneider was his 'valet'. He was a free spirit in an age that sought to extinguish such souls.

Putlitz's point of contact was one of Kell's finest appointments – a journalist called Jona Ustinov, who preferred to be known by the comical nickname 'Klop'. Klop was the father of the future actor and raconteur Peter Ustinov. The two agents met regularly, and Putlitz would tell Ustinov all that he had heard, including the latest exclamations from the Nazi ambassador Von Ribbentrop who – owing to social maladroitness – was known in London as 'Von Brickendrop'. Thus it was that MI5 learned of the Nazi enthusiasm for Edward VIII, bafflement at his abdication, and contempt for Neville Chamberlain; it was also from this source that MI5 understood that Germany was certain to attack Russia, regardless of any non-aggression pacts.

There was jeopardy in this for Putlitz, not least when he was recalled from London and sent instead to a legation in The Hague. Ustinov contrived to land himself a job for a newspaper there. If either had been caught by the SS, the consequences would not only be hideous for them, but also disastrous for MI5; anyone with even the strongest will would in the end inevitably give details away to interrogators.

At the outset of war, this became horribly apparent in what became known as the Venlo Incident. Two British agents, Captain Sigismund Payne Best and Major Richard Stevens, both based in The Hague, were lured into a trap by German counter-intelligence in November 1939. They were told that a cabal of German officers were opposed to Hitler and wanted – if the Führer were to be overthrown – to start discussing possible peace terms with Britain. It was a trick.

Together with a Dutch agent, Best and Stevens drove to the border with Germany, to a small town called Venlo. It was there that the ambush took place: the British agents were captured and remained prisoners until 1945. What's more, under interrogation, names of their fellow agents were disclosed. It was an extremely bitter blow to MI6 and Quex.

However, Quex did show some remarkable foresight that was to prove crucial to the later course of the war: in 1938, he bought a rather ugly country house in Buckinghamshire that had belonged to the Leon family. It lay halfway between Oxford and Cambridge, and was a forty-five-minute train journey from London. In anticipation of war, and an instantaneous Blitzkrieg, he was going to set his brilliantly mercurial codebreakers up in a new secret base called Bletchley Park.

In this slightly more open age, the Secret Intelligence Service has opened the files on its original 'C's and on MI5's Vernon Kell. What had begun as a vaguely amateur operation had by the Second World War unquestionably become more effective. They had turned spying into a profession, as opposed to a hobby for political extremists and eccentrics. Mansfield Cumming brought a sort of optimism to what had previously been the murkiest of trades, and it was Hugh 'Quex' Sinclair who ensured – even if MI6 had not been particularly successful in countering the rise of fascism – that at least the work of his better agents was taken seriously by a Whitehall machine that had previously been sceptical.

And so the puzzles in this section will have a flavour of that sharpened professionalism: inventive logic tests that require disciplined thought and rigorous application.

1

HEARD ON THE TUBE RAILWAY

First Lady: 'And was he related to you, dear?'
Second Lady: 'Oh, yes. You see, that gentleman's mother was my mother's mother-in-law, but he is not on speaking terms with my papa.'
First Lady: 'Oh, indeed!' (But you could see that she was not much wiser.)
How was the gentleman related to the Second Lady?

2

SIR EDWYN DE TUDOR

Sir Edwyn de Tudor needed to rescue his lady-love, the fair Isabella, who was held a captive by a neighbouring wicked baron. Sir Edwyn calculated that if he rode fifteen miles an hour he would arrive at the castle an hour too soon, while if he rode ten miles an hour he would get there just an hour too late. Now, it was of the first importance that he should be a success, and the time of the tryst was five o'clock, when the captive lady would be taking her afternoon tea. The puzzle is to discover exactly how far Sir Edwyn de Tudor had to ride.

3

THE MILKMAID PUZZLE

Here is a little pastoral puzzle that the reader may, at first sight, be led into supposing is very profound, involving deep calculations. You may even say that it is quite impossible to give any answer unless we are told something definite as to the distances. And yet it is really quite 'childlike and bland'.

In the corner of a field is seen a milkmaid milking a cow, and on the other side of the field is the dairy, where the extract has to be deposited. But it has been noticed that the young woman always goes down to the river with her pail before returning to the dairy. Here the suspicious reader will perhaps ask why she pays these visits to the river. I can only reply that it is no business of ours. The alleged milk is entirely for local consumption.

Draw a line from the milking-stool down to the river and thence to the door of the dairy, which shall indicate the shortest possible route for the milkmaid. That is all. It is quite easy to indicate the exact spot on the bank of the river to which she should direct her steps if she wants as short a walk as possible. Can you find that spot?

4

A PLANTATION PUZZLE

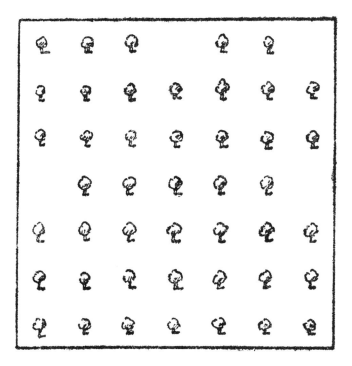

A man had a square plantation of forty-nine trees, but, as will be seen by the omissions in the illustration, four trees were blown down and removed. He now wants to cut down all the remainder except ten trees, which are to be so left that they shall form five straight rows with four trees in every row. Which are the ten trees that he must leave?

5

TURKS AND RUSSIANS

On an open level tract of country a party of Russian infantry, no two of whom were stationed at the same spot, were suddenly surprised by thirty-two Turks, who opened fire on the Russians from all directions. Each of the Turks simultaneously fired a bullet, and each bullet passed immediately over the heads of three Russian soldiers. As each of these bullets when fired killed a different man, the puzzle is to discover what is the smallest possible number of soldiers of which the Russian party could have consisted and what were the casualties on each side.

6

THE DISSECTED CIRCLE

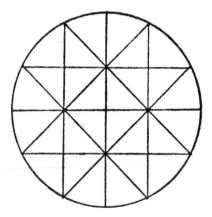

How many continuous strokes, without lifting your pencil from the paper, do you require to draw the design shown in our illustration? Directly you change the direction of your pencil begins a new stroke. You may go over the same line more than once if you like. It requires just a little care, or you may find yourself beaten by one stroke.

7

THE MONK AND THE BRIDGES

Below you will see a rough plan of a river with an island and five bridges. On one side of the river is a monastery, and on the other side is a monk in the foreground. Now, the monk has decided that he will cross every bridge once, and only once, on his return to the monastery. This is, of course, quite easy to do, but on the way he thought to himself, 'I wonder how many different routes there are from which I might have selected.' Could you have told him?

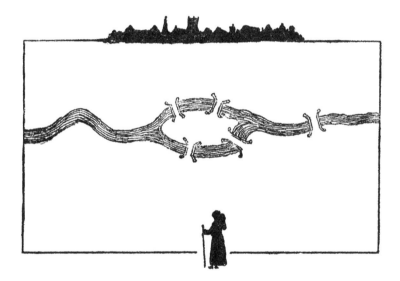

8

THE EIGHT STARS

The puzzle in this case is to place eight stars in the diagram so that no star shall be in line with another star horizontally, vertically, or diagonally. One star is already placed, and that must not be moved, so there are only seven for the reader now to place. But you must not place a star on any one of the shaded squares. There is only one way of solving this little puzzle.

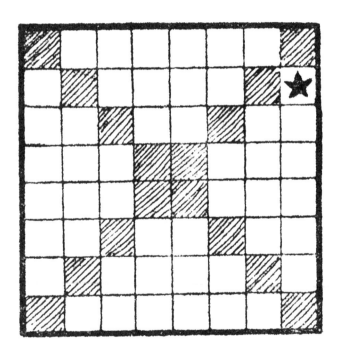

9

THE LANGUISHING MAIDEN

A wicked baron in the good old days imprisoned an innocent maiden in one of the deepest dungeons beneath the castle moat. It will be seen from our illustration that there were sixty-three cells in the dungeon, all connected by open doors, and the maiden was chained in the cell in which she is shown. Now, a valiant knight, who loved the damsel, succeeded in rescuing her from the enemy. Having gained an entrance to the dungeon at the point where he is seen, he succeeded in reaching the maiden after entering every cell once and only once. Take your pencil and try to trace out such a route.

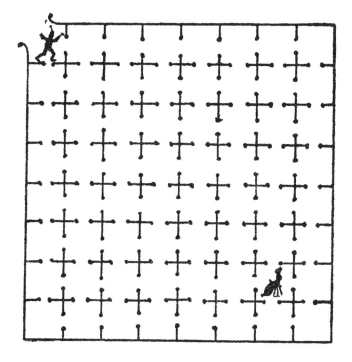

10

THE DOVETAILED BLOCK

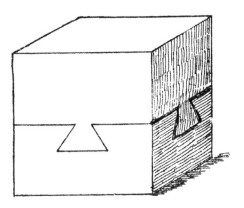

This curious mechanical puzzle consists of two solid blocks of wood securely dovetailed together. On the other two vertical sides that are not visible the appearance is precisely the same as on those shown. How were the pieces put together?

CHAPTER FOUR

LONDON CALLING

In an age of sleekly super-encrypted satellite communications, it's difficult now to imagine a time when a simple radio transmitter could change the course of history.

But for the Secret Services in the Second World War, it was messages sent over the airwaves that would cement one of the most brilliant deceptions ever carried out: an operation which saved untold numbers of lives. The radio transmissions in question were made in 1944 in the months leading up to D-Day, the Allied invasion of Europe.

It was a triumph not only of ingenuity, but also dry-mouthed nerve, with the consequences of failure too appalling to dwell on. It also – in a curious way – underlined the centrality of the humble radio set not just to the war, but also to all espionage operations generally, deep into the 1950s and 1960s.

So the puzzles in this chapter are themed around such coded transmissions, some using the actual messages sent into Nazi Germany in order to make the enemy look the wrong way. What is doubly pleasing about the story of secret radio operations is that it combines the raw courage of agents out in the field, who knew that to be captured with such equipment could mean swift death, and the bespectacled boffin enthusiasm of the technicians back in Britain who were consistently refining the technology and seeking novel new ways to disguise it. This was an arena in which geeks could be heroes too.

The radio deceptions concerned were centred around one of the most brilliant schemes ever pulled off by MI5: Operation Double Cross. As the Second World War progressed, the department – now run by Sir David Petrie, following Churchill's insistence on Major

General Kell's retirement – had taken the most agonising care to reel in double agents who were commissioned to transmit duff intelligence back to their apparent spymasters in the German Abwehr.

First among those was a man called Arthur Owens from Wales. A small businessman with Nazi sympathies, he had had contact with the Germans as the war broke out. Some of his letters were intercepted by MI5 and the choice was put to him: work as a double agent or face a grim penalty. So began the tactic of sending snippets of false intelligence via coded radio messages which would be decrypted by the Abwehr, the German secret service.

Other double agents came to be drawn in, with codenames like TATE, SUMMER and TREASURE. But the most fantastically effective of all was a man who in all fairness had only ever intended to be a single agent, against the Nazis, from the start.

Juan Pujol García, born in Barcelona in 1912, had lived through the horrors and outrages of the Spanish Civil War, and he was fixed upon helping to fight Nazism. He tried to made proper contact with British intelligence figures in Madrid throughout the Civil War but, perhaps through mistrust, he was rebuffed. What Pujol did next was breathtakingly audacious.

As the wider European war broke out, he instead offered his services as a spy to the Nazis. Pujol told the Abwehr that he would travel to Britain and from there he would provide them with much-needed on-the-ground intelligence. The Abwehr were a little hesitant about him too, but then they agreed. Pujol was given basic training, plus also the Abwehr guide to Britain, including ports and other points of military interest.

Shortly afterwards, Pujol sent his first few dispatches to his new 'masters' – but they were works of fiction. Far from landing on English shores, he had not made it any further than Portugal, and for his 'intelligence' he had cribbed from the Abwehr materials provided, adding inventive (and madly inaccurate) details of his own, such as the fact that Glaswegians would 'do anything for a litre of wine'.

Eventually, Pujol succeeded in drawing the attention of British intelligence, and now, having at last travelled to Britain, he became

'Agent Garbo'. Garbo was drawn into the web of the 'Double-Cross' system: the plot to use double agents to feed plausibly incorrect information to the German war machine.

He started by writing letters. Garbo informed his Nazi contacts about the sort of camouflage on the ships leaving Scottish ports as the war intensified, and how such markings suggested these vessels were heading to the Mediterranean (they were not). However, by 1943, radio transmissions were deemed to be more effective for conveying fake intelligence. By 1944, the proof of their effectiveness was greater than anyone in Allied Command could have dared hope.

As the Normandy landings were being planned, a shadow operation had begun, with Garbo at the centre: a series of radioed, encrypted reports to his Abwehr handlers in Madrid giving fragmented scraps of intelligence about British and American army movements on the South Coast. For a lie to work, it must have a coating of the truth. And so, according to Garbo's reports, there seemed to be signs in Kent and Sussex of an enormous influx of Allied soldiers. The presence of American military seemed especially heavy, he reported. And yes, in reality, there were numbers of new military arrivals in these southern counties – but that was not the only area in which they were congregating.

The Abwehr in Madrid faithfully relayed this intelligence to Berlin. It seemed to confirm German suspicions that when the Allied invasion came, it would be via Pas de Calais.

Garbo was sending about four radio messages a day in the months and weeks leading up to 6 June 1944. Everything he recorded was carefully impressionistic, either gathered by himself or by one of the wholly fictitious network of twenty-seven sub-agents that he claimed he had dotted around England. And as the Abwehr assembled his confected jigsaw of intelligence titbits, the picture that seemed to emerge was that FUSAG – the First US Army Group – was converging on Dover under General Patton (they were doing no such thing). Accordingly, German defences around Calais were hugely bolstered, with troops and tanks being pulled in from other areas.

The risks of this deception were quite enormous; one slip, one hint of suspicion, and the real force – actually gathered in the south-west of England and preparing for the landings at Normandy – might well, as intelligence historian Professor Sir Harry Hinsley remarked, 'have been thrown back into the sea'.

Astoundingly, there did not even seem to be a glimmer of disquiet on the German side. And as D-Day dawned, and the Normandy invasion began, Garbo added a final brilliant flourish: a message to his German handlers that the action at Normandy was simply a diversion, and that those even mightier forces of FUSAG, poised at Dover, were about to make that voyage via the Pas de Calais at any moment. Thus it was that the bulk of the German defences largely remained where they were, while the real invading Allied army managed – after furious battle and immense sacrifice – to establish the all-important bridgehead that would mark the beginning of the end of the Third Reich.

Also contributing to the wireless triumph of D-Day was a secret platoon of radio enthusiasts. These were boys and older men who – in the early days of the conflict – had been noted for their fanatical interest in the science of transmitting and receiving, and who had frequently built their own sets. This clandestine network, assembled by MI5 and run under the aegis of a special offshoot, MI8, was referred to as the Voluntary Interceptors.

As the extraordinary events unfolded, the radio enthusiasts were intercepting German communications, catching messages both coded and clear, and sending all intelligence on to their superiors; this way, the authorities could get a strong sense of what elements of the deception were still working, and what elements seemed to be fraying. It was, in a sense, the enemy's running commentary: and thanks to years of patient work and experience, the Voluntary Interceptors could even tell individual German radio operators apart. Anyone who transmits has an individual style, much as everyone has an identifiable gait, or voice; by tuning in to regular frequencies, the Voluntary Interceptors came to know these Nazi operators, in a sense, and got to the stage where they even knew when they were on the move towards fresh zones of conflict.

As with many aspects of the secret state, there was something attractively offbeat about the Voluntary Interceptors, and how they were co-opted into this deeply clandestine work. South Londoner Ray Fautley was seventeen in 1941 and by that age he was addicted to the technology of radio, happily working ten-hour days and a six-day week at a radio workshop in Morden. Even an extraordinarily close shave in the Blitz (one minute he was talking in an office, the next the office was hardly there) didn't shift Ray's focus.

One evening after a long working day, the doorbell of his family home in Tooting rang. Standing in the porch was a man in a suit and a bowler hat; he wanted to speak to Ray. And what is more, he wanted to do so privately.

They went through to the parlour and before there was any further conversation, the bowler-hatted gentleman – from the radio security department of MI5 – asked Ray to put his signature to some pieces of paper. The seventeen-year-old was signing the Official Secrets Act. Now he was under a legal obligation to say nothing about what was to follow.

It was, in essence, a daydream come true: doing vital work for the war effort that happened to be the thing that he most enjoyed doing. At first, the idea for the Voluntary Interceptors was that they should help in tracking down illicit and unauthorised transmissions emanating from within Britain, and which might be presumed to be the work of spies. But as it became increasingly clear that most spies had already been detected or rounded up, the Interceptors were instead to monitor enemy frequencies across the water. This was espionage from home: when Ray Fautley finished his day's work in Morden, he was obliged to put in two hours on the new radio that was provided for him, and which was kept concealed in his parents' front parlour.

He was also given forms and envelopes – the forms for noting all the translated Morse that he had picked up (most often he would have transcribed encoded messages in groups of four or five letters) and the envelopes for sending these forms on to a large anonymous house in High Barnet on the edges of north London, where the analysis would begin.

Ray Fautley was very proud to have been selected. His parents were aware that he had been given some job to do but they did not know what – nonetheless, they were clearly very proud too. There was only one serious moment when his cover was almost blown. Ray had told his girlfriend Barbara that henceforth they could only ever see each other at the weekend; he could not tell her it was because of his secret work. Barbara grew increasingly impatient and peevish about this treatment and clearly started to harbour suspicions.

One midweek evening, she presented herself at the front door of the Fautleys and, upon being admitted and before anyone could stop her, she opened the parlour door and marched in. She was greeted with the sight of her boyfriend hunched over half-hidden radio equipment with headphones on.

She screamed, for she had made the instant assumption that Ray was an enemy agent. Barbara turned and ran from the house, with the intention of alerting the police. Ray had to grab his headphones off and sprint out of the house after her. Not even the local policeman was allowed to know anything about the work he was doing. Ray caught up with Barbara and managed to mollify her with a yarn. Some years later, he married her. Only a great many years after that could he confess what he had actually been doing in the parlour that evening.

In contrast to this, there were some diplomatic staff around the world who considered the use of secret radios to be in breach of the essential rules, war or not; who believed that such hidden technology was in some way dishonourable. Brigadier Richard Gambier-Parry was the ebullient, bullish and hugely popular figure drawn in to MI6 partly to counter this absurd fastidiousness. His role was to make sure that agents out in the field not only had the finest equipment but also to ensure that communications back with home base were as smooth as possible.

Gambier-Parry was an Old Etonian who had been with the BBC

in its very early days, and had also worked with radio firms Pye and Philco – his enthusiasm for the technology was every bit as fervid as that of lads such as Ray Fautley. His department set up base in a rather pretty early nineteenth-century house in Buckinghamshire called Whaddon Hall.

The work done here was crucial, providing the foundations for British espionage across the world. It was through here that decoded intelligence from Bletchley Park was transmitted out to generals in the Middle East and the Far East. It was also from here that agents everywhere from Riga to the dusty hills of Albania were kept at the end of a secret radio lifeline. Gambier-Parry must have been taken with Whaddon Hall, for as well as working there, he decided to live there too.

It was certainly a grander proposition than the base for another intelligence branch called the Radio Security Service. RSS figures such as Hugh Trevor-Roper – who enjoyed pursuits such as fox-hunting – were startled to find at the beginning of the war that their headquarters was in the middle of Wormwood Scrubs prison in west London. When the conflict was declared, the incarcerated residents of the Scrubs had been evacuated to prisons in the country, as a precaution against any Blitz; as the convicts moved out, so the genteel men and women of the Radio Security Service moved in and found themselves tackling codes amid echoing cells and brick walls painted olive green.

In the aftermath of war, as the intelligence agencies renewed their focus on the Soviet Union, the use of radio for transmitting secret messages acquired a baroque and sometimes rather creepy dimension. As the Cold War set in, broadcasts started emanating from the East that anyone at all with a radio in the UK could tune into – but no one ever knew what these transmissions meant.

The most sinister of these regular nightly broadcasts became known as 'The Lincolnshire Poacher'. It always began with the first two bars of the above named English folk tune, which went: 'Oh 'tis my delight on a shining night / In the season of the year / When I was bound apprentice in famous Lincolnshire / 'Twas well I served my master for nigh on seven years . . .' What then followed was a woman's voice, sharp with aristocratic Received Pronunciation. And she would read out groups of numbers, in fives. So you might simply hear her intoning: '6 – 2 – 8 – 1 – 9' followed by other different combinations.

There were other regular broadcasts of this nature to be found elsewhere on the shortwave dial, being transmitted either from Russia or within countries that were under communist influence. The most immediate and obvious theory was that these radio codes were intended for deep cover agents working within western European countries. The numbers were essentially encrypted instructions, and encrypted call signs. Without access to the code keys, they were all but impossible for anyone else to decipher.

Among those in the know, these strings of numbers read out without any tone or passion, and interspersed with fragments of random and esoteric music, acquired a sort of spooky cult appeal. The very unknowability of their meaning gave them an eerie depth.

Curiously, today, even in this age of Skype and the internet, there are still mystery radio broadcasts out there. One, known to its devotees as 'the Buzzer', has been pulsing out from somewhere near St Petersburg since the mid 1980s. It is even more puzzling than the numbers broadcasts: this comprises a monotone drone, which is occasionally cut across by something that sounds like a distant ship's horn, and which even more occasionally is interrupted by a man speaking in Russian and saying apparently random things such as: 'the red typewriter', or 'the bullfrog in the corn'. One theory has it that if this broadcast were ever to end, it would be the sign that nuclear war was either about to, or had just, begun.

Another more winning theory is that even today, radio has a supreme advantage over mobile telephones, because although everyone can hear radio transmissions, no one can trace for whom they are intended – quite unlike the long trail of data that even the simplest e-mail or call generates. And thus, if a catastrophic conflict were to break out and internet connections were disrupted, these radio frequencies – safeguarded and kept active by continuous broadcasts – could be mobilised like any weapon, and used to send instructions to agents all over the world.

And so it is that the puzzles that follow have a distinct flavour of shortwave signals and careful tuning: no matter how dated such things might seem in a digital era, radio continues to pose its own fresh and engaging challenges for all levels of espionage.

1

A LONDON LOCATION

Here are three messages broadcast on the radio. The seemingly random words are clues to a location in London where a meeting has been arranged. Where is it?

PAROLED CALIFORNIAN CABARET

CORONA ALES

BRAZE GUN LESIONS

2

DART WORDS

Two keen radio enthusiasts like to meet up for a game of darts in the local. They both like codes and word games, and they have added some letters in numbered spaces on the board. The aim is to throw three darts and try to form words. On one night, a mutual lady friend wants to join them. The first player isn't too keen, and in his practice warm-up leaves his friend a clear message.

The player throws the regulation three darts but he takes five turns. He scores three-dart totals of 26, 18, 18, 10 and 43. He only scores 9 once and that was with his sixth dart. He hits no doubles or trebles and in every three-dart throw he hits different numbers.

What was the message?

3

FIND THE AGENT

Agents had, and still do have, names by which they are known and identified by the secret services and fellow operatives. In the Second World War, Spanish agent Juan Pujol García was known as Garbo. In the following extracts from broadcasts, the name of the agent is hidden three times in the bulletin or narrative in some shape or form.

1   It was a very regal occasion as the procession proceeded down The Mall. The weather was glorious, the sun shone and the rain of earlier in the day abated. Everyone was on view as royals and dignitaries, in the full glare of publicity, smiled and waved to the crowds. And what large crowds they were. Thousands pushed and jostled to see the carriages drive by.

Agent's name begins with E.

2   The boys had been warned time and time again. The cliff path was precarious to put it mildly and it would only take a minor slip for someone to fall on to the rocks below. Unfortunately, boys will be boys, and they were known frequently to wander off from the advised route. Fortunately, the warden of the nature reserve was a sympathetic chap with children of his own so offered a friendly word rather than a telling off.

Agent's name begins with A.

3 She felt quite nervous as the day dawned when the expedition would begin. No one could ever accuse her of being short of ideas as she had a very lively imagination coupled with a practical streak. Putting her fears aside she prepared as she had been instructed during the long hours of training she had received. She was guarding an important person, whose aides would assist in a crisis but the final responsibility was hers.

Agent's name begins with S.

4 The informer had a very good memory and stored all the information in his head. Writing notes down was not an option – far too dangerous. It was essential to have sorted all the items of knowledge to his own satisfaction before the meeting in the remote café by the sea. As his guest for the evening strode in to the secluded venue, he knew exactly what he was going to reveal.

Agent's name begins with D.

5 A last-minute change of plan was decided upon. It was often a problem to inform those who needed to know of things relating to new developments. In times of crisis, safety is an integral part of operations and no one's life should be put at risk. A number of agents on the home front have been put on stand-by, alerting those in the field that they should be ready to be on the move.

Agent's name begins with T.

4

ITMA

ITMA was a hugely popular radio programme first broadcast by the BBC in 1939, the year war broke out. *ITMA* is an acronym for *It's That Man Again* – 'that man' being comedian Tommy Handley who presented the show.

You are searching for a radio frequency. In the puzzle below there are a series of acronyms for you to unravel. To give you a further clue, each involves a number, either directly named or by a unique reference – for example, D I A W is 'days in a week', i.e. 7. Once you have worked out the answers take the highest and lowest numbers, and add them together to come up with the radio frequency you need to tune into.

1   T T D O C

2   L O A C

3   W O T A W

4   B S O A C B

5   L I T A

6   D I A L Y

7   P I A Q

8   M I A H

9   D I A R A

10 D I A R A T

5

GOLF, CHEESE AND CHESS

		CHEESE					CHESS SURNAME					GOLF CODENAME				
		CAMEMBERT	CHEDDAR	EDAM	STILTON	WENSLEYDALE	BISHOP	BLACK	CASTLE	KING	WHITE	BIRDIE	BUNKER	EAGLE	FLAG	IRON
FIRST NAME	ANGELA															
	BILL															
	CAROL															
	DAWN															
	EDWARD															
GOLF CODENAME	BIRDIE															
	BUNKER															
	EAGLE															
	FLAG															
	IRON															
CHESS SURNAME	BISHOP															
	BLACK															
	CASTLE															
	KING															
	WHITE															

FIRST NAME	CHEESE	CHESS SURNAME	GOLF CODENAME

The Government Code and Cypher School, or GCCS, carried out vital work from Whitehall and later Bletchley Park as the team managed to decipher and understand coded radio messages. The GCCS became affectionately known as the Golf, Cheese and Chess Society.

Five colleagues all have a different favourite cheese. They all have chess-related surnames and each has chosen a golf-related codename to be used in their work.

Use the information below to match all the information about the five friends. When you find a positive piece of information put a tick in the appropriate place in the upper grid. Write an X when you find a piece of negative information. Cross-refer all this information to complete the lower grid.

1 Edward is not the person codenamed Iron whose surname is Black.

2 The person with the surname Castle likes Camembert and uses the codename Flag.

3 Angela – codenamed Birdie – chose Cheddar. Her surname is not White.

4 None of the ladies likes Edam. None of the gentlemen selected the codename Eagle.

5 Stilton is the favourite of the lady with the surname Bishop. This is not Carol.

6 Bunker is the codename adopted by Bill.

6

LYRICAL

Songs were part and parcel of radio broadcasts during the Second World War and often provided a much-needed boost to morale during the dark days of the conflict. Noël Coward was an actor, playwright, composer, director, songwriter, lyricist and musical performer. In 1941 he penned a song in praise of London and all Londoners, from whatever walk of life they came from.

Unfortunately someone has written these words from the song so that they are almost unintelligible. Are they in a different language? Crack the code to reveal the words.

Emvur' syiBc lmiut sziyc omuur sriec smius stiac nmcue stioc umguh seinc imnug

sFirc ommut shiec Rmiut szitc omtuh seiAc nmcuh soirc amnud sCirc omwun,

sNioc tmhui snigc emvue sricc omuul sdioc vmeur sriic dmeu,

Tshie cpmru isdie comfu Lsoin cdmou nsTio cwmn.

7

SOUNDS FAMILIAR

Listening to messages is quite a skill as many wartime radio operators found. There are no visual clues to help you understand the meanings. Solve the groups of clues below to reveal linked messages. Take care though; how are you going to record the answers? Some words sound the same but are spelled differently and have totally different meanings.

1 Dried fruit
2 Vend
3 Playing area in tennis

4 Heaviness
5 Consumed
6 Noblemen

7 Money voucher
8 Paper
9 School resident

10 Nut
11 Perfume
12 Number in a quartet

13 Passage between church pews
14 Opposite of left
15 A pair
16 Religious song
17 Hostelry
18 Have information
19 Aromatic herb

8

THE KING'S SPEECH

In his 1939 Christmas radio broadcast, King George VI made a moving speech. By cracking the word code can you decipher what he said? All we can tell you is that, the King always comes first, and that the letters Y and Z remain the same.

R / L B V / Y B R P / G Q / R S / F R L A.

V B / X R L L M S / S B J J / V F R S / G S / V G J J / E P G L D.

G C / G S / E P G L D Q / N B R X B, / F M V / S F R L I C T J / V B / Q F R J J / E B.

G C / G S / E P G L D Q / X M L S G L T B A / Q S P T D D J B, / V B / Q F R J J / P B K R G L / T L A R T L S B A.

CHAPTER FIVE

THE BRAIN DRAINERS

No matter how sophisticated our times may seem, no matter how acutely attuned we think we are to what is true and what is false, the straightforward lie remains a potent weapon for aggressive spies in every land. There has been a foul assassination, say, possibly of a baroque nature: the drip-drip trail of twinkling radioactive material can be detected leading away from the scene of the crime. But in response to the outcry, the accused spies – and their government – will unleash a subsequent volley of deliberate lies.

The aim is not so much about denying culpability as about creating confusion and encouraging dissent. It is a technique with both a rich history and a number of unintended consequences. So to reflect this, the puzzles in this section will largely be logical enigmas, challenging you to find the true answer in amid barrels of red herrings.

Curiously, social media has made one of the oldest varieties of secret conflict into one of the most effective. Much these days is said about cyber warfare, involving young people being paid to create and maintain 'bots' – online identities that seek to generate fogs of confusion over any issue touching on the nation they work for. There are also cyber attacks on governmental and corporate computer systems, not so much for the purpose of stealing secrets as finding ways of rendering those systems inoperable. Yet strip away the keyboards and the smart phones and you find that in essence, this is still very much the realm of sabotage and propaganda that has been at the core of espionage operations since the nineteenth century.

Such techniques – the aim to destabilise an enemy nation by affecting the thoughts and emotions of its people – reached a high point during the Cold War. One senior politician, Richard Crossman, later to serve in Harold Wilson's Labour cabinet, became something of an authority on this after his experiences in the Second World War. He had been involved in Allied propaganda efforts in the 1940s aimed at Germany, which sometimes came in the form of radio programmes. After the war, Crossman became interested in propaganda techniques evolved for use against countries in the Soviet Eastern Bloc.

The Americans, in particular, were very keen on broadcasting to countries like Czechoslovakia and Hungary through the medium of Radio Free Europe and Radio Liberty. No disc jockeys and pop: this was a serious enterprise aimed at serious-minded young people in Eastern Europe who, if they tuned in at all, would have to do so very furtively. These stations carried news of anti-communist protests and meetings, and interviews with those who had crossed over to the West; to be caught listening to such material would have invited a prison sentence. Sometimes these radio stations seemed interested in fomenting further protests and even uprisings: the civil unrest in Hungary in 1956 that was so implacably and ruthlessly put down by the Soviet authorities was thought, in part, to have been sparked by American broadcasts.

What Richard Crossman vehemently disapproved of was the fact that these stations occasionally seemed to suggest that if the young people in Soviet bloc countries stirred themselves into action, then the military of the West would be poised to come to their aid. This never would have been the case. Such action would in essence have been the start of a Third World War. Crossman felt there was something both dishonourable and sinister about encouraging young people into what might be a suicidal course.

In Britain, there was (and is) the BBC World Service, always regarded in the highest ethical terms – its journalists interested not in crude propaganda, but in unvarnished truth. But even here, during the Cold War, there were some disputes: not broadsides from enraged

Soviets, but rather complaints from the Foreign Office. It was felt at some points that the BBC World Service was in fact not being hard enough on the Soviet Union and indeed might even be said to have an intellectual interest that might look more like sympathy than hostility.

But whether information comes in the form of a superbly balanced examination of the facts, or simply a brute statement about the harsh nature of oppressive regimes, in the end it can all be used as propaganda by those in power. And this type of psychological warfare was seen – in the espionage world – as the realistic way to fight the Cold War. After all, the conflict was fundamentally about ideologies, and so the aim was to make the population over the border become more drawn to the ideological stance that their governments opposed.

As the Cold War went on, psychology seemed to move to the core of hostilities. There was particular fascination, in the years following the Korean War, of the effect upon some of the young British and American men who had been taken prisoner in Korea and subjected to intensive 'education'. The term 'brainwashing' was first used in the west in the early 1950s – the word itself was said to have a Chinese origin from a character meaning 'wash-brain', incorporating the idea of cleansing the mind. In any event, during the Korean conflict, senior British and American military figures were confounded by the phenomenon of their own young soldiers appearing to be seduced by communist thinking. There was something almost occult about the way that their very personalities had appeared to change.

But perhaps the authorities found the obvious truth too startling to swallow: rather than these young apostates having been subjected to stressful mind-bending ordeals, or torture, or hypnosis in rooms with multi-coloured lights, what had happened was that they had in fact developed a natural sympathy with the Koreans. It was found that many of the so-called brainwashed prisoners were young men who had come from industrial working-class backgrounds. And so when they were out there on the other side of the world, being held in POW camps in an agrarian society completely different to anything they had seen back home, what actually occurred was something that very frequently happens with the young wherever they are: a tendency to idealise, especially when faced with the ascetic poverty of rural life. The young soldiers found the lives of the rural Koreans inspirational.

Was this what had happened to a young man who – just a few years later – would betray Britain and its secret services in the most spectacular way? George Blake was among those taken prisoner in the Korean War; he had been in a diplomatic party, which was the cover for his MI6 position.

Unlike the Cambridge Spies, Blake did not come from a comfortable public school background. Born in Rotterdam and educated in Egypt, Blake returned to the Netherlands around the time that the Second World War broke out. He was a secret courier for the Dutch Resistance, and when he and his family came to Britain, he enlisted with the Royal Navy, becoming a sub-lieutenant. In 1944, he was drawn into the secret services and took a crash course in Russian at Cambridge. He was ferociously intelligent and clearly effective. No one had any suspicion at all that following his release from Korea, he had agreed – quite wholeheartedly – to work for Russia's KGB.

And how had this happened? What made Blake switch allegiances so dramatically? He was later to claim that his thinking had been turned – while a prisoner – when watching the American 'Flying Fortresses', or war planes, roaring overhead and bombing the crops and villages of the poorest Koreans. That vision, he said, of an enormously rich and powerful force unleashing apocalyptic firepower without either thought or mercy or compassion was to have a deep and lasting effect on him. He claimed that he knew from that point that the Americans were the side to be resisted.

So his career as a double agent began. And Blake's greatest (or most infamous) coup involved the secret Berlin tunnel – which in itself was going to turn into a very good illustration of the importance of psychological warfare.

In the mid 1950s, in the partitioned city of Berlin (yet to be divided by the vast concrete wall but nonetheless jagged with barbed wire and tension), a team of British engineers and boffins were working deep underground. They were busy installing futuristic equipment to eavesdrop on all secret Soviet communications by tapping cables on the East German side. This tunnel, brilliantly dug out under the cover of a 'warehouse' on the West German side of the patrolled border, ran about 1,500 feet across the frontier, where the Soviet telephone cables could be accessed. Only a very few knew anything about it. But MI6 agent George Blake was one. And he in turn told his Soviet contacts.

The Soviets initially took no action; they let the British continue burrowing and bugging in the soon completed tunnel system. This was partly to protect their agent Blake: if they had 'discovered' the tunnel before it was properly operational, he would have been narrowed down as the source and at that point, he was too valuable. Indeed, to make the bluff even more authentic, the Soviets did not even tell the East German authorities that they were being bugged; if they had done so, there would have been an unusual silence which would have puzzled the British and the Americans.

Once the tunnel had been operating at full capacity for a few months, however – and some time after George Blake was transferred to other territory – the Soviets seized the moment for what they thought was their own psychological coup.

A team of East German diggers 'happened' across the tunnel from their side of the city; and once they had done so, they invited the world's press to photograph what they saw as the perfidy of the West's spying operations. The reasoning was that the CIA and MI6 would end up looking sinister and aggressive, and the East Germans would seem wronged innocents.

It did not quite work out that way; in fact, psychologically, the episode turned out to be a double coup for the Western alliance: first because in the time before the 'discovery', they had harvested reams of genuine intelligence; and second because the press reaction seemed to be one of some amused admiration. In those early days of the Cold War, the psychological impression was given that America and Britain were assured and ahead of the game, at least when it came to electronic surveillance.

However, this was a great deal more than could be said for the human side of intelligence. As we will see in a later chapter, the West had by this time been dealt several very serious blows involving traitors who were much more shocking – and in some cases – a lot less fathomable than George Blake. Blake, incidentally, was finally unmasked as a double agent in the 1960s. He was sentenced to forty-two years in prison, managed to escape from Wormwood Scrubs in 1966, defected, and has lived out his life in Russia since.

Quite aside from traitors, the psychology of secret agents has long been a source of fascination because those agents themselves are required to have a keen eye for the striations of human nature. MI5 trainees in the 1950s and 1960s were instructed throughout training in the best way to detect those who were hiding communist beliefs, or who were susceptible to advances from the opposing side. But what of their own natures, and what sort of psychological profile was best suited to the tasks in hand?

Aside from loyalty and a sense of humour and a certain nimble-wittedness, there also had to be bravery and a talent for acting. The ability to carry off a faked identity requires psychological deftness and indeed a certain amount of empathy.

By contrast, impetuosity is a trait that is most unwelcome; first because it can yank judgement off course and second because it draws attention. The successful secret agent is a person who understands how not to be noticed, and indeed how to be underestimated. The sort of coolness required to be able to completely merge into the background might equally be found in those with high levels of patience and very little sense of having to prove something – and equally in those who are simply sociopathic enough to focus like lasers on achieving success.

Above all, the most brilliant agents have always been those who – having infiltrated whatever form of society required of them – succeed first of all in offering sympathetic ears to others and then, having done so, invisibly persuading those others to offer them more information.

So in this section, many of the puzzles will require that greatest psychological asset of patience; the answers are there to be teased out but only when you are thinking coolly. There is an additional difficulty though: many of these puzzles are set against strict time limits, the aim of which will be to demonstrate if you can hold that psychological resolve level as the clock clicks ever downward.

1

CAFÉ SOCIETY

There are sixteen cafés in this quarter of Paris, each marked with a circle on the grid below. Le Café des Partisans is marked in the bottom right-hand corner of the plan.

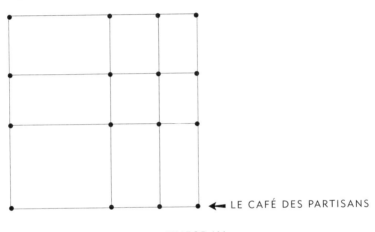

← LE CAFÉ DES PARTISANS

TUESDAY

Starting in Le Café des Partisans, our surveillance expert has to walk to all the cafés on the plan through the maze of streets in this part of the city. There are many routes, but he must walk in straight lines without covering the same street more than once, and must visit each and every café. Time is of the essence so he must make these visits with the smallest number of changes of direction. How many will there be in total? Leaving the first café counts as a change of direction.

WEDNESDAY

He suspects someone is on his trail. His starting point is once again Le Café des Partisans. Again he must visit each café. Again he must walk in straight lines without covering the same street more than once. However this time he is keen to change direction as often as possible to lose anyone who might be following him. How many changes will there be this time?

2

LYING LOW

Keeping a low profile and avoiding suspicion is part and parcel of observational work. This may be for a matter of hours or a matter of months. Use all the coded letter cards to fill the grids so that every row and column will spell out a word. The HI card has already been placed to start you off. When completed, the top rows spell out the instruction that means the observation work is at an end.

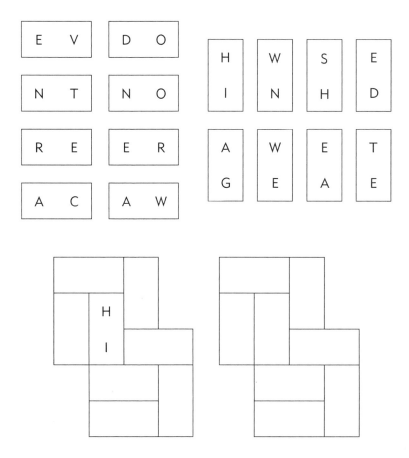

3

MINDGAMES

Someone has been playing mindgames. Twenty-four words are written seemingly at random. However they can be rearranged into six groups of four words. You must play the mindgame as the groups can be looked at from many different angles, but there is only one definitive grouping.

KISSING	LOVE	BOX	STRINGS
GOLDEN	ROSE	WINGS	PITCH
RACKET	BALL	BREAK	PIT
CUE	SET	MENIN	NET
SCORE	SERVE	SAFFRON	BRASS
CROCUS	POCKET	VIOLA	BRANDENBURG

4

PLAYING FOR TIME

Six different agents each meet their team leader in a West London bar. The counter-espionage team knows that meetings are planned for successive days but the timing at first is a mystery.

Each agent has vital information but it is the final meeting on the final day that is the most important.

From intelligence sources, the counter-espionage team have discovered four possible timings for the final day. However one member of the team has noticed a pattern emerging and thinks she can predict the exact time of the final appointment on the final day when vital secrets will be handed over. Have you spotted what she spotted?

Monday – meeting at five minutes past noon
Tuesday – meeting at three forty-five
Wednesday – meeting at ten fifteen
Thursday – meeting one fifty-five
Friday – meeting nine twenty

When is Saturday's meeting: three thirty? Ten past eight? Twenty-five past eight? Quarter past nine?

5

SECRET SERVICE

The Secret Service or SIS is what this book is all about. Jetting around the world to different destinations and criss-crossing countries and continents gives a hint of the thrill of the enterprise.

To solve this puzzle you must fit all the listed place names below back into the two grids. Words are written a letter at a time in the six spaces around a number. You can start in any space adjacent to the number and words can go either in a clockwise or anti-clockwise direction. You must decide which way they go. One person is starting out from LONDON (written clockwise), with stop 11 their final destination. Another person is starting a return journey from MOSCOW (written anticlockwise) with stop 1 in the same grid the final destination.

Where in the world will the two agents finish?

ALEPPO	MADRAS
ATHENS	MANILA
BERLIN	MOSCOW
BREMEN	OSTEND
DIEPPE	POLAND
GALWAY	PRAGUE
ISRAEL	SWEDEN
KUWAIT	TAHITI
LAHORE	VERONA
LISBON	VIENNA
LONDON	ZAGREB

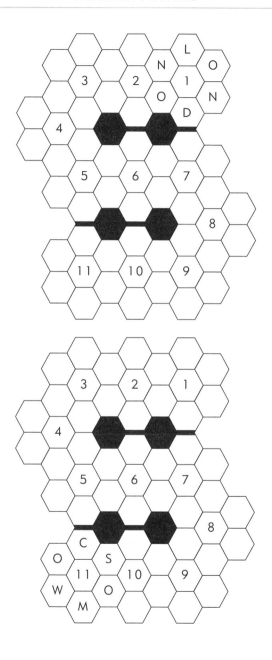

6

RENDEZVOUS

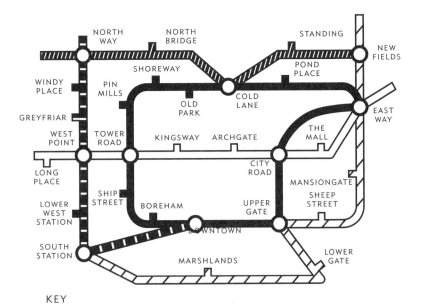

KEY

▭	CITY LINE
■	INNER LINE
▨	OUTER LINE
▤	LINK LINE
▧	SOUTHERN LINE
◯	STATIONS WHERE YOU CAN CHANGE LINES

Four agents have planned a secret rendezvous. They have agreed to meet at the same station on an underground network. Alicia sets off from North Way, Boris from New Fields, Katarina from South Station and Dietrich from Lower Gate.

1) If they all travel the same number of stops, what's the least number of stops that will enable them to meet up? Which station is the meeting point? No one can revisit a station.

2) They all decide to travel seven stops each. Again, no one can revisit a station. At which station will they meet?

7

SHIPS THAT PASS . . .

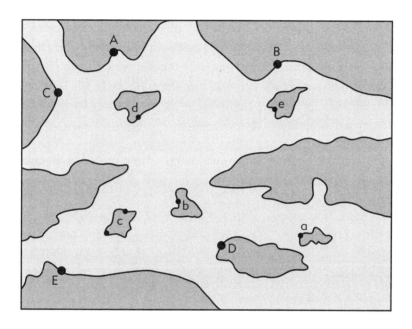

Five boats set sail from the mainland ports, which are represented by capital letters A to E. Each boat is heading for the island which is marked by a matching lowercase letter.

Can you plot the ships' courses so that none of the routes will ever cross?

8

WOULD I LIE TO YOU?

It comes to your notice as head of the department that certain classified information has been passed on to the enemy. You know that you are not the guilty party. Only the four people who work in your departmental office could have access to the highly sensitive information. You call your team in to your office. You explain the situation and then quite bluntly ask them for their immediate response.

Andrew came straight to the point. 'Brenda is responsible,' he said.

Brenda put the blame on her female co-worker. 'Daisy is passing on secrets.'

Charles was keen to defend himself. 'I am not the spy.'

Daisy spoke last, and although clearly annoyed by being accused, she remained calm. Her response was, 'Brenda told a lie when she said I am passing on secrets.'

Only one of your colleagues is telling the truth.

So, who is passing on secrets?

CHAPTER SIX

DOUBLE AGENTS? (SIX DOWN, TWO LETTERS)

Of all the extraordinary emergencies that MI5 has had to deal with over the years, the crossword conundrum was among the most startling. The alarms went off at one of the most acutely sensitive moments in modern history – the weeks and days before the D-Day landings of 1944 – and the mystery has continued to perplex and enthral over the last seventy-five years or so. Were undercover agents using the *Daily Telegraph* crossword to send crucial intelligence to the Nazis?

The story began in the early spring of 1944, with an agent with MI5 who could not let the day pass without completing his crossword. The clue for 17 across that day was four letters and not cryptic: 'One of the U.S.' The answer was Utah. Nothing at all remarkable about that. But a few days later, the answer to another clue was 'Omaha'; like 'Utah', a codeword for a beach to be used in the Normandy landings. A few weeks after this came 'Neptune': codeword for the naval operation; then a few days after that, 'Mulberry', which was the name of the innovative floating harbours that were going to be deployed. Another crossword clue a day later carried the answer 'Overlord' – codeword for the entire operation.

This surely went beyond curious coincidence. How could there not be sinister work afoot here? Of all the secrets at that time, the proposed beach landings were the very gravest; only a very tight and select circle was privy to the plans. So what was going on and how

97

was this most establishment-minded newspaper somehow being used as a vehicle for diabolical espionage?

MI5 launched into action, amid a real sense of suffocating anxiety: should any of these plans be transmitted to the enemy by whatever means, the invasion of Europe might fail. Enquiries to the *Daily Telegraph* revealed that all the crosswords in question had been compiled by one of their most valued setters: Leonard Dawe, who was the headmaster of a minor public school, the Strand, in Surrey. Dawe had been devising puzzles for the newspaper since 1925.

The agents swooped. But as they led Leonard Dawe out of the main school building and into the back of their car to be driven back to London, the scene was witnessed by the head boy, and – perhaps illustrating how very difficult it is to keep anything secret – he and his fellow pupils appeared to divine that their headmaster had been pulled in over some security issue.

Leonard Dawe was absent for three days. When he returned to the school, he naturally said nothing. The boys in his charge were left to their lurid speculations, though as one commented many years later, no one could believe that Dawe was involved in any kind of scandal – after all, he was a member of the local golf club.

About fifteen years later, in the late 1950s, Dawe, still quite reticent, agreed to be interviewed for the BBC, because this curious crossword clue conundrum was still being regularly mentioned in newspaper articles. Of the three days when he was in the care of MI5, he simply said that they turned him 'inside out' and that Melville Jones, another *Telegraph* compiler detained by MI5, had also been 'put through the works'. The extraordinary fact was that both men were completely blameless; they must also have been utterly horrified at any suggestion that they would so blithely betray their country to the Nazis.

MI5 had to agree: they had done nothing wrong. And so, Dawe told the BBC, they decided 'not to shoot us'.

Yet there was still the mystery: how did so many of these vital keywords turn up as crossword answers at this crucial – and still top-secret – moment of history?

It was a *Telegraph* correspondent who tried to get to the bottom of it. Not long ago he spoke to some family members of those who had boarded at the Strand school during the war. There were some stories passed on from old boys to their sons. And one such story was this.

In the spring of 1944, the build-up in numbers of British and American soldiers in the home counties was particularly conspicuous, and there was a base for US and Canadian soldiers near the Strand school. Fascinated by the soldiers' presence – plus also the suggestion of weaponry and adventure – some boys managed to slip out of school to the military camp to engage them in conversation about their heroic deeds. The soldiers were apparently amused by this and – in the anxious monotony of the wait for D-Day – they were clearly glad to be able to talk to young people who had no doubts about their courage.

And so, as the story goes, these US soldiers also passed on to the boys what they knew about the planned invasion. Talk was peppered with the key words. The boys, heads reeling with excitement, trooped back to school, and of course all the conversation was of nothing else.

Here is where Leonard Dawe came in: the avuncular headmaster had a habit of outsourcing some of his crossword compiling. He would challenge his boys to come up with good, intriguing and varied answers – to which he would then devise suitably cryptic clues. One boy – who appeared to have the most retentive memory, and the sharpest taste for mischief – made suggestions of the codewords he had heard from soldiers. And so they became woven into the crosswords, with Dawe having no idea of their real significance. In later years, as soon as the weight of what he had done became apparent, the boy was reportedly beyond horrified. He was said to have confessed to the headmaster and the headmaster, equally horrified, told the stricken boy to burn any notebooks or diaries that might contain the terms.

It is a very beguiling story, all the more so for being difficult to believe. Putting to one side the undeniable fact that the Americans really were shockingly bad when it came to security and keeping secrets, there remains the question of how it was that ordinary soldiers knew about these highly classified codewords.

Now some might say that codewords by themselves are useless to the enemy: even if they could deduct that 'Omaha' and 'Utah' were supposed to be beaches, what then? But with a network of intelligence, such codewords might be cross-referenced against others: this was a technique honed to a fine art by the codebreakers of Bletchley Park, for instance. So the highest military authorities around Churchill would surely never have allowed these key words to be allowed into everyday usage. The risks were already stratospherically high.

But if not that, then what? It has also been pointed out that twenty years later, in the days leading up to the escape from Wormwood Scrubs by previously mentioned double agent George Blake, there was a 1966 *Times* crossword that appeared to contain clues and answers amounting to a premonition or, more pertinently, a message to the prisoner, who was himself a crossword addict: among the answers were the antique term 'runagates' (meaning runaway or escapee), 'gaol' and 'artillery'. Blake's accomplices were in a car parked in Artillery Lane, just off Wormwood Scrubs. Again, the intelligence services found themselves interviewing a slightly bewildered and perfectly innocent crossword compiler.

So was it all just an awful coincidence, after all? In the wake of the war, the *Daily Telegraph* itself returned to the subject. It is said that in 1982, the then editor Bill Deedes became hugely anxious about something similar happening with the crossword just as Britain prepared to go to war with Argentina over the Falkland Islands. The clues were scoured for any codewords that might have crept in. None were found.

So here then are some of the historic *Daily Telegraph* crosswords from 1944 that triggered the original alarm. The keywords including 'Omaha' and 'Utah' should now serve as something of a head start!

1

2 MAY 1944

On the day that the first crossword to contain a top secret D-Day codeword was published, the unaware readers were absorbing news of US 8th Army bombing raids on Nazi marshalling yards in Belgium and France. The crossword clue in question featured the code for the beach that the US 4th Infantry Division was to land on.

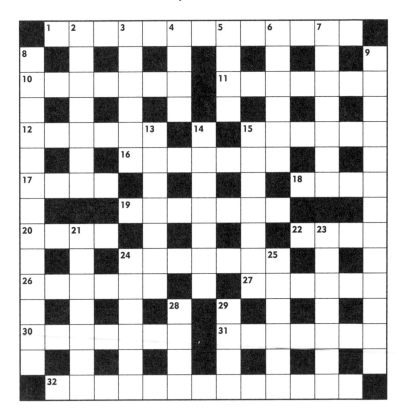

ACROSS

1. A cause of postscripts (13)
10. Very attentive commonly (3, 4)
11. A fool's weapon (7)
12. But this isn't to be bought at this shop (6)
15. Foils start this (3, 3)
16. Definite (7)
17. One of the U.S. (4)
18. Achievement that the guardians of the Tower always have at heart (4)
19. Proper behaviour (7)
20. But cook has a practical use for this old weapon (4)
22. Part of one's last will and testament (4)
24. This knight of old had a fair start (7)
26. Little Samuel has got something from the pantry to make a boat (6)
27. The ceremonious tart (6)
30. Fifty fifty (7)
31. White wine (7)
32. 'Intense matter' (anag.) (13)

DOWN

2. This probably has a lateen sail (7)
3. What all will be when the cease fire sounds (6)
4. Try the clue for 22 Across (4)
5. Derby winner or preposition (4)
6. Systematically sorted (6)
7. When this loses its tail it doesn't grow another (7)
8. He rations the port among those who want it (13)
9. The ups and downs of business (6, 3, 4)
13. Conference centre lately (7)
14. 'Sleep rough' (7)
15. Lay (7)
21. Assess (7)
23. 'Having drink taken' (7)
24. Many an oak-tree has this measurement (6)
25. This might make mad, sir (6)
28. This German island sounds of alluvial origin (4)
29. The last Alice saw of the White Rabbit? (4)

2

22 MAY 1944

The second crossword D-Day clue featured the codeword for the beach on which the US 1st Infantry was to land. That day, there was news of new types of American bombers being flown to Britain, and proposals from the International Chamber of Commerce that a post-war Europe should be seeking to eliminate trade barriers.

ACROSS

1. A shot that falls short is not thus satisfactory (2, 2, 3, 4)
9. Town of Germany (5)
10. 'Call Ina home' (anag.) (11)
11. The Derby winner to start a branch of mathematics (5)
12. Tree used in the building of the Temple (5)
15. Town to go down in times of drought (5)
17. Drink upset in 10 Across (3)
18. To get this fabulous lady just ponder (4)
19. Ecclesiastical assembly (5)
22. Its sole work is to produce some effect (5)
23. Not obsolete (2, 3)
24. Battle of the last Great War (5)
26. One probably this these represented at a 19 Across (4)
27. The start of 35 Across (it's given you) (3)
28. This worker is as good as five in the RN (5)
30. The way in which a tasty lemon might come in useful (5)
33. An overworked word nowadays for 'rate' (5)
35. This gives vagueness to place or number (11)
36. Lightweight of the animal world (5)
37. The credit for a joint thus perfectly cooked should go to the turnspit (4, 2, 1, 4)

DOWN

2. This meal would be bit by bit (5)
3. Red Indian on the Missouri (5)
4. Wine (4)
5. No small deer (5)
6. He wrote 'A thing of beauty is a joy for ever' (5)
7. By sticking to one's work (11)
8. A mere jumble of words (11)
12. At any rate a writer of music should have this to offer importunate creditors (11)
13. Kind of absentmindedness (11)
14. Gathering in which all take part (5)
15. This continental river might easily become a drain (5)
16. Sign of the Zodiac (3)
20. Displeasing (5)
21. One of the worldly wealthy (5)
25. Stands for the control of the lower Thames (1, 1, 1)
28. Well-known refusal given to the lad (5)
29. Edge (5)
31. Fish that resists your getting him his tail (5)
32. Afterwards (5)
34. This term for a European of sorts seems to be 500 years old (4)

3

27 MAY 1944

This was the day on which the codeword for the entire D-Day operation featured as a crossword clue. The public on this day, still perfectly oblivious, was reading reassuring reports of new 'rocket projectiles' being fired at enemy German ships in the North Sea.

ACROSS

1. No half-baked praise (4, 4)
5. The county of firm personnel (6)
9. Incog. (3, 5)
10. Not apparently very high-class land — (6)
11. — but some big-wig like this has stolen some of it at times (8)
13. They may send one's temperature up, oddly enough (6)
14. It serves its turn in the opening episode (3)
16. Scattered inroad to order (6)
19. He has his duty to master (7)
20. 'Die a V.C.' (anag.) (improving words to a soldier?) (6)
21. It needs Erse to slander (3)
26. Need to come to signify (6)
27. When to change to the 31 Across? (4, 4)
28. To show grief about a lady is not fruitless (6)
29. What separates the novice from the adept (8)
30. No enemy allowed a bed (6)
31. Remote terminus don't mix around here (5, 3)

DOWN

1. Cut out the chaff and do not delay victory (6)
2. The one that was left at the post? (6)
3. Hang up more than a corner (6)
4. They are probably prepared for floods in this English town (6)
6. Not prolonged enough to make the torso hot (3, 5)
7. Not a strange spirit, apparently (8)
8. Entertainment that tells one what to do at it (8)
12. This Eastern is often in a whirl (7)
15. Is familiar with the cells from birth (3)
16. Reversed in 26 Across (3)
17. Sounds a useful thing to wear, but no help (8)
18. There's no list for the ships on this (4, 4)
19. Of secret composition and not taxed (4, 4)
22. What a girl might expect if a sailor gives her the bird? (6)
23. Cool place to work in? (6)
24. Figure of speech is turned on quite a way (6)
25. Asked for convalescent patient's meal (6)

4

30 MAY 1944

Extraordinarily, following all the other clues, on this day the name given to the ingenious and secret floating harbours was featured. All as newspaper readers were absorbing the Nazis being pushed back in Italy and also reports of a forces cricket match at Lord's at which the players refused to stop for a tea interval: revolutionary behaviour!

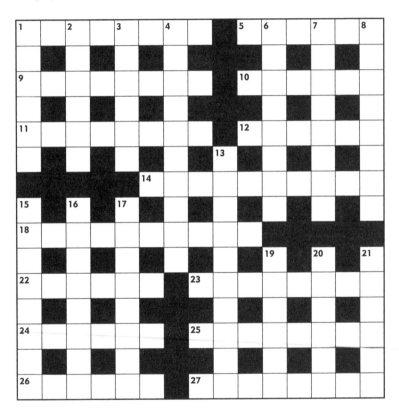

ACROSS

1. 'Wandering near her secret bower molest her ancient — reign' (Gray) (8)
5. Danger courted by billiard players (6)
9. His weapon is the pen (8)
10. Tenant of a kind (6)
11. This bush is a centre of nursery revolutions (8)
12. It is no use asking a jazz band to play this for a dance (6)
14. An early example of the NAAFI girl? (10)
18. The stronger his team the less this member of it has to do (10)
22. The dim distance (6)
23. 'Eager set' (anag.) (8)
24. The words that stick in the mouth of the sufragette who has found a husband (2, 4)
25. Courteous though exercising compulsion (8)
26. Epithet for that story of the ivy that strangled a sleeper (6)
27. An old week (8)

DOWN

1. A suitable opening word (6)
2. Not so long ago (6)
3. This great English painter does not sound like any cubist (6)
4. If there are grounds in the coffee the cook should be this and the coffee this before serving it (10)
6. Did a nose get out of order? This may be the cause (8)
7. Of various kinds as arranged (8)
8. Man's justice (8)
13. We this men's deaths; it's very sad (10)
15. 'Coasting' (anag.) (8)
16. Not the same as a liking for veal (4, 4)
17. Only on the surface (4, 4)
19. Gracious (6)
20. The kind of fence to lose colour (6)
21. The motive force for a grandfather clock (6)

5

1 JUNE 1944

When this crossword clue, the answer to which was the secret name for the naval arm of the D-Day operation, was published, the official consternation increased – yet the readers still knew nothing of any of this.

ACROSS

1. 'Lid on slang' (anag.) (but is all 15 Across so pure in speech?) (4, 6)
8. Doing nothing because there's nothing doing possibly (4)
10. The kind of constitution that laughs at doctors of the Goebbels type! (10)
11. Our supposed portion in 1940, but we never tumbled to it — (4)
12. — though coming to the this of it (4)
15. Where the work of the architect stands very high (3, 4)
18. The girl who went into her own reflections very amusingly (5)
19. You must be plumb right! (5)
20. Just a note (5)
21. Got in wrongly to the bar (5)
22. Would this problem be a sitter to an artist? (5)
23. A joint affair (5)
24. Not a forbidding hue (5)
25. She is in an ancient city (official) (5)
26. Of Eastern origin, but serious (7)
30. Cast a skin (4)
33. Points in favour of some players (4)
34. A submarine should be, of course (10)
35. He gets his wings on false pretences (4)
36. Where to look for Maud's boyfriend? (6, 4)

DOWN

2. Sign of appeal to men (4)
3. Cause of the hidden hand? (5)
4. Like a bear with a sore head (5)
5. He may be like the curate's egg, good in parts (5)
6. Outcast agents of fickle chance (4)
7. Flower one might well salute (4)
9. End of a term for losing cohesion (8, 2)
10. Those working in it are quite sunk in their work (6, 4)
13. It may be seen at the front at feeding time (5, 5)
14. See printer for an adventure (10)
15. Britannia and he hold to the same thing (7)
16. Sphere of 15 Down (5)
17. An exclusive notice (4, 3)
20. The roots of smokers' pleasures (5)
27. It comes from the rates – blooming scandal! (5)
28. Choice of directions of tongue (5)
29. Was an arm, or might support one (5)
31. No good man will live up to it (4)
32. Shoot to spot (4)
33. Finished! (4)

CHAPTER SEVEN

DEADLIER THAN THE MALE

The young woman and her male colleague had ventured deeper into the building than they had perhaps intended. It was a featureless office block in the featureless Russian town of (then) Kalinin, 100 miles north of Moscow, in the mid 1950s. On the ground floor, the woman and the man had seen banks of telephones intended for the use of local citizens, and specifically for the purposes of reporting neighbours for dissident behaviour.

It was the woman who had found the staircase and she and the man were now at the end of a corridor on the first floor, looking at rows of shut doors. Suddenly, one of those doors was opened. A female Soviet official stepped out into the corridor, looked at the woman and the man, thought for a moment – then stepped back into the office and closed the door.

The woman was the first to indicate that she and her male colleague should make a bolt for it. Two British agents in the heart of the KGB's local headquarters; capture did not bear thinking about.

The idea was that once they were out of the building, the couple could blend into the crowds on the street; their pursuers would lose them in the hubbub. As they got outside, however, they saw that the streets were actually near empty. They were aware of a commotion going on in the building behind them. The only alternative was to run.

A flight through cobbled streets in the cold air of the Russian spring; the woman realised that rather than getting lost, and run the risk of accidentally doubling back on their pursuers, she and her colleague should follow the hill down to the River Volga.

Then as they stood on the bank, they knew what they had to do. With the approaching clamour not far behind, the young woman unbuttoned her skirt, and jammed it into her attaché case; the man removed his trousers, doing likewise. And then they both jumped into the water.

By her own account, the shock was so intense it was almost like a heart attack; the river was not frozen, but was still freezing. Nonetheless, the agents allowed the strong tide to carry them around the bend of the river, far from their baffled pursuers. There they scrambled up the bank on the other side, spent an icy few minutes drying off, then dressed.

This was one episode in the life of a pioneering female MI6 spy called Daphne Park. Later in life, she was to become Baroness Park of Monmouth, the principal of Somerville College, Oxford. But for many decades the full extraordinary range of her career lay in the shadows of the Official Secrets Act.

And so inspired by not only her story, but also the surprising careers of so many pioneering female agents, the puzzles in this section owe something to the observation made that women make better spies because of their aptitude for multi-tasking. Here, single objectives will be complicated by several other factors, as you negotiate your way through tests involving everything from bandit-haunted jungles to the fire of revolution.

Born in England in 1921 but brought up in Tanzania, Daphne Park learned fortitude early; for a while, she lived in a mud hut. Returning to Britain as a teenager, she studied at Oxford and – as the Second World War broke out – was gripped by a determination to be as active as possible. Through her contacts, she learned that it was possible for a woman to join the Special Operations Executive. And after the war, there was no possibility that she was going to let this new life go. So Daphne Park stayed on with MI6.

Her physical courage was noted early on – and she later said of herself that her tendency towards rotundness helped as well: wherever she was posted, she was not seen as being 'sinister'.

She learned Russian, and soon was travelling through the Iron

Curtain under the identity of a diplomat. But her career was to take her further yet: a posting to East Africa at the time when Harold Macmillan's 'winds of change' were starting to blow, and independence from colonialism was coming for so many countries. The aim was to try and ensure stability when all was changing and the possibilities of violent revolution and civil war were ever present. Daphne Park was posted to the Congo, during the period when the Belgians were withdrawing. At the time, she drove a Citroën 2CV; this was an extension of the idea of not looking sinister.

But it also made her vulnerable, at a time when the dusty roads were haunted by gunmen. There was one occasion when gunmen literally tried to haul her out of the car via the roof. She claimed that she got stuck and started to giggle. As a result, the gunmen were metaphorically disarmed, and started to laugh too. On another occasion, mentioned earlier, it was a proffered bottle of whiskey that came to her rescue. Daphne Park not only had the sort of intelligence that would enable her to see the meaning of codes; she also had the rarer gift of being a perfect judge of human behaviour, calculating instantly how best to win over those who might potentially kill her. The most serious moment came when she was again seized and this time thrown into a roadside pit as the prelude to an execution. This time, she saved herself with calm talk and reason. The ability to keep up that level of sangfroid made her a source of wonder among colleagues.

Yet despite the presence of Park and other pioneering women operatives such as Jane Sisemore, the secret services could be frustrating for female recruits. In the 1960s, a young Stella Rimington joined MI5 and found even when she became a junior assistant officer that women were expected to do the more subordinate jobs. For instance, if there was a safe house to be used for valued contacts, it was the women who were asked to go on ahead and make sure that it was clean, tidy, and that there was plenty of milk in the fridge.

Added to this was what might be seen as another regressive element: the type of women recruited to work in the more clerical departments. In a habit left over from well before the war, these

SECRET AGENT BRAINTEASERS

tended disproportionately to be upper-class debutantes, strings of pearls tucked into their jumpers and fresh from lunchtime dashes around Harrods. This meant that women entering the service from other backgrounds might have perceived not only the barrier of gender but also of social class, hindering chances of promotion.

The services were apparently sensitive to this though and indeed, with the advent of the 1975 Sex Discrimination Act, there were departments that were enthusiastic early adopters of equality. Obviously, the harrumphing old guard did not disappear overnight. But for instance, over in MI6, the abilities of Daphne Park were fully recognised and, after a spell in Hanoi during the Vietnam War, she rose to head her own department, becoming an agent runner. And though change was not instantaneous, it is notable that when the newly appointed Dame Stella Rimington became the first ever head of MI5 to be named in public, in 1992 – before that, newspapers and television would never have considered revealing such a state secret – the surprise was more about the revelation itself than about the fact that the head of domestic intelligence was a woman.

This was still a landmark moment; Dame Stella was the first woman in the world to be made head of any secret service. None of her colleagues assumed this was down to positive discrimination; her long career with MI5, which had begun in the late 1960s, was marked, as her superiors said, with decisiveness and confidence. She had monitored possible communist infiltration in various 1970s left-wing hot-spots including the University of Sussex and the National Union of Miners. She was now also facing new responsibilities for countering the murderous activities of the Provisional IRA. What did not help her as she started her new role was the fevered public interest in every aspect of her life.

Indeed, Dame Stella had been very much against having her identity revealed in public at all; the publicity was a modernising stipulation that had come down from Downing Street. Originally it was only supposed to be her name that was made public, but everyone in Whitehall should have understood that the newspapers would be desperate for a photograph. And with the deductive, puzzle-solving skills of the spies themselves, Fleet Street photographers and journalists succeeded in tracking down her home address, the fact that she was separated from her husband, the branch of Marks and Spencer that she favoured and even her bank account number – which enabled one larky hack to pay in a deposit, along with a reference saying 'From KGB chief'.

There was very much less about her formidable skills at burrowing down into real-life espionage conundrums, and for fathoming and calculating the next moves of the enemy based on analyses of intercepted messages and carefully followed movements. Instead, Dame Stella seemed to tap into a very old public fascination with women spies and how they were perceived to be almost a completely different species from the male variety. Even the impeccably politically correct broadcaster Jon Snow proclaimed that he was surprised to find that Dame Stella was not 'Rosa Klebb'.

In the public imagination, there were two sorts of female agents. 'Rosa Klebb' was the creation of Ian Fleming, a KGB officer described as a faintly toad-like lesbian with a strong streak of sadism. But countering this was the glamorous woman spy who used her sexual allure to trick secrets out of beguiled men. This was the template that – way back in 1915 – allowed the woman known as Mata Hari to gain such worldwide notoriety. The fact that Mata Hari's real story was painfully sad – an exotic fantasia that led inexorably to her own violent death – did nothing to tarnish the legend.

Her real name was Margaretha Geertruida Zelle; she was born in the Netherlands, though would later claim to be a 'Javanese princess', raised on the banks of the Ganges. Her background was middle class, but a series of calamities led her to answer a newspaper advertisement from a British military officer looking for a wife and based in the Dutch East Indies. Her marriage to Rudolph MacLeod was abusive: a litany of violent alcoholism, syphilis and child mortality. When they split, Margaretha allowed her husband to keep custody of their surviving daughter.

When she returned to Europe, she regenerated: Margaretha now became 'Mata Hari'. She had acquired an extraordinary skill for dance, which she deployed in routines that were both flagrantly erotic but also curiously modernist. Many of the dances involved the removal of various garments, leaving her in a bra glittering with jewels. But the act was not remotely regarded as smut; instead, the orientalist element led to Mata Hari being feted by the intellectual classes as well as aristocratic society. She performed in the grandest theatres in Italy and Paris; the persona that she had constructed became a mask that could never be removed.

Though there were intense love affairs, Mata Hari was never the wanton woman of later legend. But it was this idea of her hold over men that set the tragedy in motion. As the Great War enveloped France, she was persuaded by the French secret service to spy on the Germans. Having been born in the Netherlands, Mata Hari was still at liberty to cross borders that were closed to others. And so her espionage career began.

At some stage, she also received an offer from the Germans, effectively making her a double agent. And though it was never apparent that she had ever revealed anything much more than could be overheard in town squares or read in local newspapers, this was still a position of some jeopardy.

Sailing to England, she was detained and interrogated by MI5; on her release, she travelled to Spain. There, her German military contact sent coded messages back to his superiors not only with intelligence, but also with enough clues for the French codebreakers intercepting these messages to identify her as 'Agent H-21', the source of these secrets.

On the move once more, Mata Hari was arrested by the French. She pleaded her innocence but after prolonged interrogation appeared to make a qualified confession that she did in fact spy for the Germans. The qualification was that she had never given them any useable intelligence.

It was too late; the web was spun around her. In 1917, the French had suffered incalculable losses in the blood-soaked trenches, and the trial of Mata Hari appeared to make her the ideal emblem of the sinister enemy: a wicked woman who would stop at nothing to betray so many innocent men. She was sentenced to be shot. It was said that she faced the firing squad with quite extraordinary courage, refusing a blindfold and waving to her lawyer before her hands were tied. In the end, she was a victim of a sort of public hysteria; there is little indication in this sad story that she had much agency in her own life.

Later female agents were grievously under-estimated. One such was Jane Archer who, in the years just before the Second World War, had proved an extremely valuable recruit to MI5. Her interrogation techniques elicited key details that might on the face of it seem innocuous but on closer investigation would prove to have great significance. And she was extremely alert to the smallest anomalies.

But she was also ferociously outspoken, and when MI5's first Director Vernon Kell was replaced at the outbreak of war by Jasper Harker, whom she regarded as useless, she said so, volubly. This behaviour was seen as intolerable. Jane Archer was fired from MI5.

Happily, she transferred to MI6; even the male-dominated, clubland-oriented security services could not afford to lose such talent. And it is perhaps the greatest backhand tribute to her powers that in the post-war years, as relations with the Soviet Union froze over, one key figure regarded her as a very serious danger.

Jane Archer was by that time working under MI6 officer and double agent Kim Philby, and Philby knew how, a couple of years previously, she had been in on the interrogation of one General Krivitsky, who had defected from Stalin's Russia. Amid all the gobbets of information that the general offered was one that particularly piqued Jane Archer's interest: it concerned a young journalist in the pay of the Soviets and reporting directly to them, who had gone out to Spain to cover the Civil War.

Philby knew that it was impossible that Jane Archer had not followed this up; she would have soon discovered that her boss, Philby, had been a journalist for *The Times* out in Spain. He equally knew that Jane Archer's suspicions of him would have been knife keen – and completely correct.

Fresh jeopardy for Philby was presented in the late 1940s by the detention in Canada of a Russian called Gouzenko; here, once again, it was clear that an incisive interrogation would yield new intelligence. Kim Philby became ever more fearful that his own very active treachery would be revealed. So when he was consulted about whether it was best to send Jane Archer or another officer, Roger Hollis, over to Canada to conduct the interrogation, Philby ensured that it was Hollis who was selected to go. Jane Archer would have been more incisive and dogged – indeed, Philby later confessed in his memoirs, she would have been a very bad enemy to have.

Through more manoeuvrings, Archer was transferred again, back from MI6 to MI5, sidelined by unwitting (and witting) superiors. However, she did not remain on the sidelines for long. Archer was working in the department responsible for security clearances and she was soon on the trail of other Cold War traitors; in a later chapter, we will hear more not only of the other Cambridge Spies but also the nuclear scientist, working at the very heart of the British nuclear establishment, who was determined that Stalin's Russia should have atomic weapons.

For the moment though, Jane Archer stands as a good emblem of the two most vital qualities required for solving real-life espionage enigmas: the courage never to have one's own suspicions and convictions knocked off course by the confusion and malice of office politics, and also the sort of diamond-bright memory that can recall the smallest fact, no matter how innocuous, from years previously.

So the puzzles in this section partly take their lead from these attributes, plus also the essential ability to juggle several problems simultaneously. And this is to say nothing of identities. It is interesting to see that one of Dame Stella Rimington's abiding passions away from her work was for amateur dramatics: she took roles in a wide variety of productions. It is safe to assume that one who is trained to see beneath constructed identities might have something of a knack for constructing many identities of her own.

DEADLIER THAN THE MALE

1

A SERIES OF TYPING ERRORS

Every man knows that women are often skilled in multi-tasking. In this section not only do you need to solve individual puzzles, you must also deal with another challenge . . . multi-tasking indeed! Can you pick up a clue in each puzzle in this section to supply you with the first name of the agent you will meet once the whole section is completed?

Our typist in the department has made a series of errors when typing up some notes. Or has she? Can you sort out the information?

He learned to play a grind piano.

I am spending my holiday in an exclusive hovel.

Stately home ovens for everyone.

Dairy meals are eaten in the kitchen.

Untie tomorrow! Can't wait.

A match for soldiers is part of their training.

2

CROSS PURPOSES

Clever women have worked in the world of espionage for many years. Daphne Park was an exceptional lady in this field. Her name is written downwards in the grid below. Solve the clues and slot the answers to read across into the grid using the letters in Daphne's name to help you. When you have done this, cross-refer to pick out the coded letters to spell out the name of a book with a Daphne Park link.

	A	B	C	D	E	F	G
1	D						■
2	A						■
3	P						
4	H						
5	N						■
6	E						
7	P						■
8	A						
9	R						■
10	K						

Most populous city of Pakistan and capital of Sindh province (7 letters)

Its Tsar was overthrown in 1917 (6)

Imaginary line around the centre of the earth (7)

The Netherlands (7)

River rising in the Black Forest, which flows into the Black Sea (6)

Port on the west coast of Italy (6)

Second largest continent (6)

The _____ Spring was a thwarted 1968 movement in Czechoslovakia (6)

Mozart and Strauss were residents of this country (7)

Bird with brilliant feathers and a tail that expands like a fan (7)

Now cross-refer: use the letters that have the following grid references.

B6 / B9 / F7 / E5 / F4

_ / _ / _ / _ / _

E3 / B2

_ / _

C8 / C5 / G10 / F1 / D9

— / — / — / — / —

3

COFFEE SHOP

Evenings or weekends, four friends regularly meet in a coffee shop. One of them is very important and you must make contact with her today. They are queuing for a coffee and cake and it is the friend who is fourth in the queue who you must get in touch with. Who is she? Use the clues below to help you find out.

Alice, Camilla, Lizzie and Mollie are ordering a Mocha, a Latte, a Cappuccino and an Americano. Foodwise there is a choice of flapjack, croissant, cupcake and muffin and they all choose a different treat.

Lizzie is immediately behind whoever has ordered a mocha with a flapjack.

The person with the Americano is at the front of the queue.

The two at the back of the queue haven't ordered a cupcake.

The person with the latte is not in front of the person eating the muffin, who ordered a Cappuccino.

No one is ordering a coffee or food with the same initial as their name.

4

DEAR PAM

Revelations about emotions are often found in poetry. A lady member of the SOE receives the poem below, addressed to 'Dear Pam'. Understandably she is deeply moved by the sentiments expressed. However, in reality, the poem describes a wholly different kind of 'move' she needs to make. What must she do, where must she go and when?

The birds in the sky
        How high they do fly,
Evening draws near
        And soon you'll be here.
Tell me it's true,
Remind me that you
Everlasting love faithfully vow.

All day I shall wait,
        Tomorrow's too late.
No tears now, just laughter
        Our happy ever after.
Our just you and me,
Never parted we'll be.

5

KEEPING WATCH

Prevention is a key part of counter espionage work. A member of the surveillance team is keeping watch on a group of five people who meet to tend their allotments. But is that all they do? Could they be up to no good? Each gardener specialises in the cultivation of something different and spends a different number of hours per week on his/her allotment. We give you a view from above of their respective plots which are marked A, B, C, D and E.

Gardeners: Ms Birch, Mrs Forrest, Mr Hedges, Mrs Lawn, Mr Woods.
Growing: Alpines, Fruit, Herbs, Shrubs, Vegetables.
Hours per week: 7, 9, 12, 14, 18.

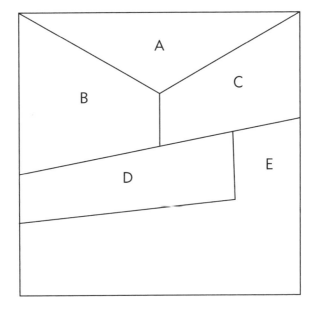

The two gardeners who spend least time on their allotments are the two key people you and the surveillance team need to keep watch on. Who are they?

Use the information below together with the allotment plan to work out who does what.

1   Mr Hedges has a three-sided allotment on which he grows herbs.

2   The individual who grows alpines spends exactly half the number of hours on his/her allotment as the person who grows vegetables on allotment D.

3   Mrs Lawn on allotment B is not the person who grows fruit for nine hours per week.

4   Mr Woods, who of the five gardeners spends the most amount of time on his allotment, has a plot that borders just two others.

5   On one side of Mrs Forrest's allotment is the person who spends twelve hours a week on their plot.

6

LIBRARY SECRETS

Genevieve works in a specialist library. Some of the book titles are listed below. Some are exactly what they seem – library books. There are two books, however, which are used to conceal secret messages. By looking at all the titles, can you work out which books these are?

HOT TOMATO

MOUTH TO MOUTH

MY MAXIM

ON A WHIM

TOY TAXI

VOW TO MARY

WAY OUT

WHAT A MYTH

WHY TIMOTHY

7

SHADOWED

Level-headedness is a quality found in so many of the women who worked in the secret services. The plan shows a location a member of the team has never been to before. Her instructions are designed to take her the safest route to the station, as her colleagues know there is a shadow on her tail. It is important that she looks confident and decisive, and above all that she follows these instructions to the letter.

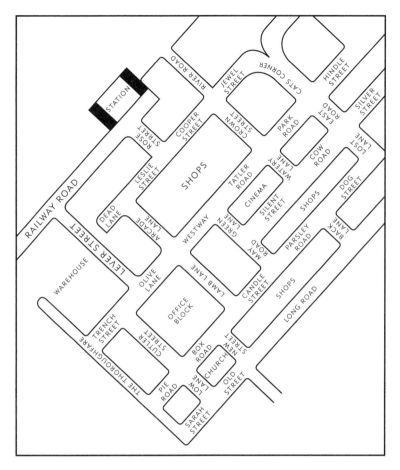

What were the instructions, and can you plot the route?

Clue 1: Visiting Westway is as far removed from orders as you can get.

Clue 2: The route takes in the animal-named places except Cats Corner.

8

WHEELS WITHIN WHEELS

Ever wondered how people were recruited to the Secret Services in their early days? It often depended on who you knew, rather than what you knew. In the 1960s, writer Charlotte Bingham took on a secretarial role in MI5. Her father was a senior officer there. In this puzzle, Charlotte Bingham's name goes around the outer edge of the wheel. Answers 1–10 are numbered, have six letters and go from the outer edge of the circle inwards. The circular answers 11–25 go clockwise, have four letters each and their clues here are in no particular order. To make things more tricky, in the list there is a single word of four letters, which will not fit. What is it?

RADIAL CLUES 1–10

1	Code	6	Teasing
2	Lie in wait	7	Revenue
3	Government	8	Led
4	Commands	9	Possessing
5	International agreement	10	Secured a boat

CLOCKWISE CLUES

Duty list	Harbour
On a single occasion	Duplicate
Thought	Subsequently
Resign	Twelve months
Female relative	Border
Written reminder	Revise
Portent	Young women presented at court
Look for	Painting, music etc

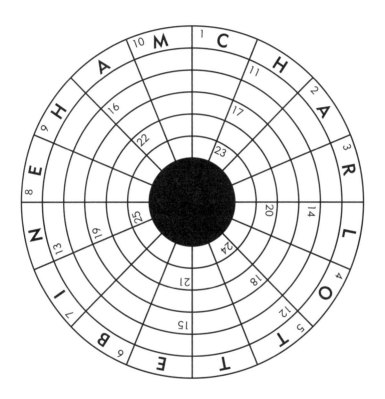

CHAPTER EIGHT

CHAPTER AND VERSE

Spying is about both surveying the world and interpreting it, prying out the hidden motives of people and the hidden meanings of landscapes. It might, for instance, involve gazing upon a desert mountain range in the glowing gold light of a sunset and understanding that buried somewhere amid that beauty is an enemy stockpile of lethal weapons. It might also be about watching a man sitting alone in a pub, pen tapping away at a newspaper crossword, pint hardly touched. You have been told that he is awaiting a contact but does his behaviour suggest that he knows he is being observed?

So it is perhaps only natural that among the very first recruits into the formalised secret service were poets and writers of fiction. Indeed, a flair for narrative is a secret service tradition that continues to this day.

As a result, the puzzles in this section will all reflect a certain literary sensibility, involving textual challenges and linguistic enigmas that require the solver to dig deep beneath everyday vocabulary to yield up the true answers.

The most famous author/secret agent is John Le Carré, still writing gripping and morally powerful fiction almost sixty years after his debut. Le Carré (real name David Cornwall) is an example of a spy who turned his experiences in MI6 in the late 1950s into a means of exploring the often desperate hinterland of human nature: betrayal, deceit, breakdown. There can be few bleaker novels in the genre than 1963's *The Spy Who Came in from the Cold*, in which the British secret service, icy with cynicism, conducts a lethal double-bluff with the East Germans across the Berlin Wall, dragging their own man Alec Leamas towards an ever more appalling fate.

It is understandable, therefore, that Le Carré has little time for the more escapist works of a man who had been at the centre of wartime naval intelligence. In turn, Ian Fleming and his creation James Bond could never have been accused of examining the tragedy of a spy's corroded soul. But Bond might instead be said to authentically represent another facet of the intelligence services and that is its absolutely unswerving loyalty to Queen and country. Bond's superior, M, although ruthless about the deployment of his 00 agents, is also nonetheless a sort of gruff father figure, and the Bond of the novels loves him dearly.

All the colourful escapades – from *Goldfinger*'s physically impossible plot to steal all the gold from Fort Knox (in the film, the plot is to irradiate it instead), to Hugo Drax's plan to use former Nazis to fire a missile at London, to Ernst Stavro Blofeld plotting to send mesmerised young women out from his Alpine lair and into the wider world with their make-up compacts filled with deadly germs – take place against the reassuring stability of a Britain that knows that only its agents can save civilisation.

Conversely, there is little sense of having to fathom secrets in Bond's adventures. Even the code-generating machine that he is after in *From Russia with Love* is purely a means of providing plot momentum. You sense that 007 would not have a fraction of the patience or the lateral skill required to actually break any codes himself.

But the secret agent has to rely on instinct as well as intellect and perhaps the most brilliant fusion of the two can be found in the life and works of the novelist Graham Greene. Greene travelled widely, venturing into the more rugged regions of South America and Africa, which few others would have found congenial. It was a result of his experience of negotiating difficult territory that he was approached to join MI6. Greene was that rare instance of a man already famous for his fiction subsequently entering the shadowed double life that his reading public would never know about.

After receiving his own bespoke training course, ranging from encryption to sabotage techniques, Greene was posted to Freetown, Sierra Leone, in the latter part of the Second World War. He spent his days gathering what intelligence he could, and his evenings relaxing in the once-grand bar of a once-grand hotel. And it was during this period that he also began to write *The Ministry of Fear*. This is one of the most abidingly disorientating and chilling – yet also quirky and witty – spy novels of all time. The novel's hero, Arthur Rowe, moves through a Blitz-torn London, propelled like a pinball through increasingly bizarre scenarios: a curiously menacing garden fête in Bloomsbury on a storm-laden afternoon in which a fortune teller persuades him to enter the 'Guess the Weight of the Cake' contest, with quite extraordinary consequences; a séance in a darkened room in Notting Hill during which one of the participants is somehow stabbed with Rowe's knife; and a murder attempt coinciding with a bombing raid that leaves Rowe's life quite literally turned upside down.

Rowe moves from crisis to crisis as though in a dream, trying to fathom why assassins would want to kill him. The diabolical plot actually involves embedded Nazi spies, secret formulas and blackmail, but the essential point is that the novel is also about the way that the world that one sees and touches and feels can still be wholly deceptive. A spy is accustomed to peering into kaleidoscopic chaos to find the true patterns.

This is arguably why a novelist like Graham Greene was such an attractive recruit to MI6. He could imaginatively summon an apparently baffling world of secrets and mysteries, and he could see the reality underneath.

All that said, spycraft is also about guile and cunning and this is perhaps why storytellers so frequently seemed to have the right sort of mentality for the work. One recent example is the best-selling novelist Frederick Forsyth. Best known for his thrillers *The Day of the Jackal*, *The Odessa File* and *The Fourth Protocol*, Forsyth was approached by MI6 in the late 1960s when he was a journalist covering the Biafran War. He later recalled that he was filing reports to the BBC plus also to his 'new friend' in the SIS. And although he was never full-time (or indeed paid), Forsyth continued the relationship throughout the 1970s and 1980s. There was one occasion when MI6 asked him to go to Communist East Germany, meet the secret contact, and collect a vital package to bring back to London.

The whole episode would have been perfect in a novel: the writer posing as a man with an all-consuming love for Graeco-Roman artefacts; the visit to the Albertinum museum in East Germany in order to view some otherwise rarely seen treasures; the trip to the museum lavatory; the package pushed under the door. Thereafter, the task was to get it back to the hotel, and then through the airport without being stopped. Forsyth succeeded.

His novels – some involving Politburo plotting and Soviet manoeuvring and the world being pulled towards a nightmare nuclear confrontation between East and West – are renowned for their accuracy and in-depth detail. Forsyth revealed in his autobiography that his friends at MI6 could be very helpful as advisers. He would, he said, sometimes send them pages from the new work in progress – not just to check the facts but also to make sure that he was not inadvertently revealing too much of the inner workings of the deep state. MI6 told him that they would let him know if he had gone that little bit too far – but in fact, the pages always came back with an enthusiastic endorsement and thumbs-up.

Yet there were a couple of much-loved authors, their works still adored today, whose own missions for the secret service could not have been more different from the fictional worlds that they created. Compton Mackenzie was the author of the Hebridean comedy *Whisky Galore* (made into one of the most popular of the Ealing comedies) and the sunny *The Monarch of the Glen* (much later a successful television series), having served some time in Greece for the nascent MI6. Meanwhile, even more strikingly, Arthur Ransome, the author of beloved children's classic *Swallows and Amazons*, was embedded as a curious kind of double agent at the heart of the Russian Revolution in 1917.

Compton Mackenzie was recruited into the service during the First World War, and was posted to Athens to set up espionage and counter-espionage operations. This was a life that he clearly relished and indeed 'C' (Mansfield Cumming) thought very highly of his output. Mackenzie was not universally popular though and there seemed to be some internal resistance to the idea of him being promoted. In any event, Mackenzie seemed rather brilliantly attuned to Mediterranean life and managed to construct a hugely effective intelligence network. After the war, he drifted away from the security services – although one way or another, he was never going to quite escape.

The most astoundingly prolific writer of everything from novels to plays to essays. Mackenzie had a seemingly inexhaustible ability to be interested in everything, from obscure methods of playing snooker to Siamese cats. But his memoirs of his spying days in the Mediterranean, *Greek Memories*, published in 1932, brought him into sharp conflict with his old department.

The difficulty was that he was accused of breaking the Official Secrets Act and identifying fellow agents. Even more shockingly, he had revealed to the world the existence not only of MI6, but also of 'C'. This was at a time when the secret services were never acknowledged out loud in any public sphere. Compton Mackenzie was facing the prospect of jail.

Before the trial, he and his legal representatives were approached by MI6; if Mackenzie would agree to plead guilty, they could ensure that the penalty would be a simple (if stiff) financial one. He duly did so – but the judge was said to be so annoyed by the manner of the government prosecutor that the fine was reduced from £500 to £100. Nonetheless, fighting the case had left the author quite seriously out of pocket – and on top of that, the first printing of *Greek Memories* had been withdrawn. A censored, redacted version would be issued some time after.

Partly in order to make some more money, and also partly to exact a satisfyingly satirical revenge, Compton Mackenzie immediately set to work on a new comic novel entitled *Water on the Brain*. In this, dimwit Arthur Blenkinsop is recruited by the secret services – or the Department of Extraordinary Intelligence – to try and effect regime change in the fictional country of Mendacia. His cover is that of a banana importer. But in the farce that follows, he ends up entangled in multiple plots. The idea, said Mackenzie, was that it might sound like some Marx Brothers comedy but quite often, the people recruited into intelligence really did get caught up in chaotic nonsense.

Meanwhile, in terms of sheer distance between fictional creation and real-life exploits, few could have matched Arthur Ransome. Or at least, this is how it seems at first glance. But did the author of the immortal *Swallows and Amazons* partly tap into a child's enthusiasm for games of espionage in this book?

Swallows and Amazons, published in 1930, was the story of two families and their children in the Lake District. As well as piratical boating games on the lakes, there were other terrific adventures, including night-time challenges on the water, missing manuscripts and over-heard burglars. Here was the idyll of the outdoors: sailing, camping, corned beef, lemonade, and grouchy adults slowly being won around.

And yet its author had, just a few years previously, led the most extraordinary, adrenaline-fuelled life as Lenin's revolution had swept through Russia in November 1917. Ransome had first arrived in the country several years beforehand in the wake of a shattered marriage, and was intent upon immersing himself in Russian folklore and legends, partly as literary inspiration. He was also filing copy for the radical newspaper, the *Daily News*. Come the revolution, he was so well embedded in Moscow that he came to know Trotsky and Radek, among other senior Bolsheviks. His second wife Evgenia was Trotsky's secretary.

Meanwhile, Ransome was also sending intelligence back to London; he was regarded as being a rather brilliant source. His position in some ways was quite extraordinary: having the trust of the Bolsheviks at a time when trust as a commodity in Russia was vanishingly rare. But the depth of Ransome's associations and indeed sympathies with the Communists did arouse some suspicions back in Britain. His supporters always reasoned that the excellent factual content of the intelligence provided had to be delicately unpicked from his very obvious sympathies. But there were others who wondered rather more darkly if Ransome could be trusted at all. What if he was the instrument of the plotting Bolsheviks, rather than a conduit of news?

But Ransome returned to London, a little after the Russian civil war, and he brought new wife Evgenia with him. His espionage days were apparently over; the future lay in his love for being on the water, and his love for writing.

And what could be further from the tumult and bloodshed and trauma of the Russian revolution than finely observed descriptions of Lake District life, plus the innocence of high-spirited children on holiday under open skies?

Yet *Swallows and Amazons* utilises many of the elements of imagination and adventure that seem to have inspired grown-up spies: islands to be explored, opponents to be outwitted, territory to be mapped, a world to be absorbed and understood. Added to this is the abiding spirit of independence, of living a life detached from humdrum domestic normality. This is a life lived beneath the stars with improvised sleeping bags.

So perhaps in one sense, Arthur Ransome's timelessly wonderful fiction is more in tune with the gung-ho spirit of spying than Ian Fleming's; indeed, his characterisations of the children seem very much more human than 007 James Bond who, despite all his cocktails and womanising, seems essentially at heart to be a wantonly destructive and disturbed ten-year-old boy.

Either way, it's clear the connection between espionage and literature is a strong one. So the puzzles in this section will reflect the sensibility of all these writers by focusing on the more literary side of the spying life – that feel and instinct for the multiple meanings to be found in even the most innocuous-seeming sentences.

1

THE LANGUAGE OF LIDO

All of the questions below are based on an invented language called Lido. Word order is different from that of English and there is no wrong or right order, so there are multiple solutions (for example, 'the man likes the rabbits' or 'the rabbits like the man'). Start by reading the sample sentences in Lido for each section and then answer the following questions.

illk etd eou – The man likes the rabbit.

las tim ord – The fox eats the chicken.

ictided illk end las – The rabbit and the chicken are playing.

laseek tim lid end illkeek – The fox watches the rabbits and the chickens.

tim end illk lided eoueek – The men are watching the fox and the rabbit.

luny las end narded illk – The chicken and the rabbit are running away.

eoueek illkeek etd – The rabbits like the men.

ivereek lid eou – The man watches the animals.

a) Give the meaning of:

    i. lided eoueek ivereek

    ii. eou etd illk las end

b) Translate the following sentences into Lido:

    i. The rabbits and the chickens like the men.

    ii. The fox is watching the chicken run away.

SAMPLE SENTENCES 2

tim hei laseek ord – The fox eats five chickens.
illkeek ean eoueek lid – Three men watch the rabbits.
illk cin icti bey – The lady plays with the rabbit.
luny tim lid eil illkeek nard – The fox watches two rabbits run away.
icti beyeek ivereek lid – The ladies watch the animals play.

c) Give the meaning of:

    i. las eou end bey lid
    ii. illkeek eoueek icti cin eil

d) Translate the following sentences into Lido:

    i. The man watches the fox and the fox watches two chickens.
    ii. Three rabbits, two chickens and the lady run away.

SAMPLE SENTENCES 3

ogge ord eou – The man eats an egg.
eil oggeek mon tim – The fox steals two eggs.
las ric eou lided bey – The lady is watching the man drop the chicken.
illk ap las nard – The chicken runs on the rabbit.
bey da monded eou oggeek – The man is stealing eggs from the lady.
kiddleek cin ivereek ictided – The children are playing with the animals.

e) Give the meaning of:

    i. illkeek orded eil timeek
    ii. lid eou oggeek ric ean tim

f) Translate the following sentences into Lido:

  i. The ladies are watching the fox steal five eggs.
  ii. The men and the children like the animals.

2

CODE POEMS

Possibly one of the more aesthetically pleasing means of encrypting messages, poetry codes were deployed in the early days of the Second World War. While lacking the head-swirling complexity of Enigma (these were devised for agents in the field to use, armed with only pencil and paper), there was a certain elegant ingenuity to them.

Here below are some poetry code puzzles that will give an idea of what it was like for agents to use such ciphers. It is all about accuracy under pressure. All you will need is pen and paper. And to imagine yourself either in some Balkan mountain cave, or deep in a forest, with the sense of time ticking down inexorably.

The method: from each poem featured, four or five keywords have been randomly chosen.

With each puzzle, write the key-words down, in block capitals, on blank paper.

Now number the letters, as they appear alphabetically. If there is more than one 'A', for instance, you number the second 'A' 2 and then the following alphabetical letter '3'. So, if the key words are, for instance, selected from Shelley's 'Ozymandias' and are 'ANTIQUE', 'WORKS', 'BARE' and 'SAND', you would write them out as below, and number them as below:

```
A  N  T  I  Q  U  E  W  O  R  K  S  B  A  R  E  S  A  N  D
1  10 18 8  13 19 6  20 12 14 9  16 4  2  15 7  17 3  11 5
```

From this, we see we have 20 letters. Now write the numbers out in a long line, as below:

1 2 3 4 5 6 7 8 9 10 11 12 13 14 15 16 17 18 19 20

Now we come to the code. As with Enigma, this would have been transmitted in groups of four or five letters. For the purposes of these puzzles, they are in four-letter groupings. And the code letters in this instance are:

TWAP FSLA NILE UHOA EWTT ELAC
DOHN HHBE SAET GSOT

Now the process of unscrambling them! We are using the poem words – and the numbers below – as the key. We are using each letter in sequence. Thus, the first letter, the A of 'antique', also happens to be number 1. We take the first two code letters – TW – split them, and place them in our new grid under number one, the T on top of the W. Now the next letter: in 'antique', the letter N is number 10. So we take the next two code letters – A and P – and on our grid, place them under 10, the A on top of the P. The next letter along, 'T', is 18. So we take the next code letters, F and S, and place them under number 18, the F on top. Continue and you will see two lines of letters being formed. And these letters, when read along, will form the secret message.

One extra complication. A time limit for each. Steadily decreasing . . .

a) Finish decoding the sentence above. You have ten minutes. (N.B. If messages came up a little short, as they often did, the left-over letters at the end would be filled in with the alphabet.)

b) Out of Shakepeare's immortal (and thus easily memorised) sonnet, 'Shall I compare thee to a summer's day?' the five key words are: 'ROUGH, DARLING, MAY, SO, BRAG'.

Here is the encrypted message, in groups of four:

IMCR TBOU CNTE TESE EIDD IPMM
VSHM HCNA EIAS IDEU IA

Can you decode the message, using the method above? Clue: An explosive emergency in a public place!

You have eight minutes.

c) From 'Pied Beauty' by Gerard Manley Hopkins, the encoded words are: 'GLORY, DAPPLED, ADAZZLE, HIM'

The encrypted message is:

UHSK NUMS UAUI TLGC SKBE NHRN
HEAT EDGB GCEY IEMO ICIP

Clue: You have to admire the diabolical ingenuity.

You have four minutes.

d) From 'The Passing of Arthur' by Lord Alfred Tennyson, the code key words are: 'WEIRD, GHOST, BIRDS, DREAM'.

The encoded message is:

LNBU ITDS EDSE EDIE NTEO
NWSU DTMI BIYS EAAS EOHB

Clue: This tells you where to look.

You have three minutes.

CHAPTER NINE

WHOSE SIDE ARE YOU ON?

In the rose-glow of the warm setting sun, deep in green Oxfordshire and near the ancient Rollright Stones circle, a young mother stepped out of the back door of her honey-coloured cottage. As the evening sky turned ruby, she made her way up to the end of the garden, took three or four stones from the wall, and retrieved a radio transmission set. Silhouetted against that red sky was the spindly mast, and the tree to which it was fixed. The woman took the radio back into the cottage, set it running, and began sending her message in coded Morse.

She was transmitting to Soviet Russia. And the intelligence she was sending was that Britain and America had jointly agreed to develop and build nuclear bombs. In the months to come, she would be sending further intelligence, provided by an atomic scientist based at the very heart of this new nuclear enterprise, in nearby Harwell.

When we now think of British double agents, the names that come instantly to mind are those of the Cambridge Spies: Kim Philby, Guy Burgess, Donald Maclean, Anthony Blunt. Yet for a time there was another agent operating with terrifying effectiveness while maintaining an ordinary guise. Her name was Ursula Beurton and she had been nicknamed 'Red Sonya'.

Double agents have been an enduring source of fascination since the beginning of the secret services – the idea of an enemy hiding in plain sight is both intriguing and unsettling. So the puzzles in this section are about tracking down the mole within. This sort of detective work is not just a case of homing in on radio signals or telephone calls, but also being able to divine truth from carefully constructed deceit.

We will of course touch on the Cambridge Spies because they continue to fascinate on many different levels. But it was agents such as Ursula Beurton and, later, Melita Norwood who arguably had the greater treacherous success. Whereas the Cambridge Spies had attracted suspicion quite early on, these two women managed largely to evade attention (in the case of Melita Norwood, this remained the case until the 1990s).

Buerton, née Kuczynski, was born in Germany; her father was a highly regarded economist. Her passion for communism developed quickly and she was a committed activist for the party throughout the 1920s. She married an architect, Rudolf Hamburger, who was also a devout communist. His work took them both to China, where he worked in Shanghai. And it was here, amid the ex-patriot social network, that Ursula was introduced to Richard Sorge. He was a full-time spy for the Soviets and he was swift to recruit her. She had a particular aptitude for complex radio work, an invaluable skill – and indeed, she was spirited to Russia for a few months intensive training in this and other technological skills.

The next move was to Switzerland in 1938. By this stage her first marriage had collapsed, and soon she met an Englishman, Len Beurton. A second wedding brought a British passport and her transplantation into the heart of an old rural community that took to her and indeed her parents with great warmth.

The move to Oxfordshire was shrewd. MI5 had moved many of its operations to the small town of Blenheim for the war. Meanwhile, the country's foremost atomic scientists were working in the laboratories at Harwell, also close by. Ursula Beurton was put in contact with one particular scientist, Klaus Fuchs, who was desperately anxious that the Russians should not be left behind in the new age of nuclear weaponry, and equally anxious that the secrets he knew should be conveyed to them.

The actions of Fuchs and Buerton, in concert, were to shape the Cold War – though they would have seen it as bringing much-needed

WHOSE SIDE ARE YOU ON?

equality of firepower, so that the ideal of communism could defend itself against the voracious forces of capitalism. What makes the story so fascinating is how two such intense and committed agents could somehow operate without being detected. Klaus Fuchs – who had also worked at the super-secret Los Alamos base when America's first atomic bomb was being developed, and used his preternaturally sharp memory and intellect to reproduce plans that he had seen there – ended up at the heart of the British nuclear establishment with no difficulty.

Equally, even with her powerful radio equipment hidden in her Oxfordshire garden, Ursula Beurton for a long time evaded attention too. On a couple of occasions, the Radio Security Service had triangulated some suspicious transmissions to the region of her cottage, yet somehow she had convinced them that such things could not possibly have anything to do with her.

Yet eventually, Fuchs and by extension Beurton were uncovered; not by investigators in England but by a brilliant cryptographic coup shared between American and British codebreakers, who had made their way into a haul of Soviet diplomatic messages. This intelligence shone a light into the depth of Soviet penetration of Britain's most secret establishments.

Fuchs at first denied all charges of furnishing Russia with atomic knowledge, then he capitulated. He was put on trial and sentenced to fourteen years in jail. Released after nine years, he emigrated to East Germany as soon as he was out. Meanwhile, Ursula Beurton had realised that the trail would lead very quickly to her, and before the authorities could make a move, she left the country with her children in 1950, never to return. She was later to receive some of the highest honours from the Soviets. In her mind, she was never a traitor at all, but rather someone who worked towards creating the perfect society.

Elsewhere, the same was true for possibly the most remarkable Soviet spy of them all. Melita Norwood was said, decades later, to have been more valuable to the Kremlin than all the Cambridge Spies put together.

Born near Bournemouth, and inheriting her parents' fervid left-wing beliefs, Norwood eventually went to work for the British Non-Ferrous Metals Research Association in the 1930s. The boring name hid the extraordinary truth: through this organisation passed all the research secrets of Britain's nascent atomic weaponry programme, under the equally flat codename 'Tube Alloys'.

Melita Norwood had already been recruited to work for a country that she had an almost religious passion for. And – taking some care – she had access to an astonishing range of blueprints in her work at the BNF. Her superiors in Soviet military intelligence provided her with the latest in miniature photographic equipment to record it with. All the material she managed to capture was passed on to her Soviet controller in London.

Again, in the strictest terms, what she did was the highest treason: this was handing over the plans for vital weaponry to the enemy (even if the Soviets were temporary allies during the war). The truly amazing thing was this: Melita Norwood was only finally revealed to be a spy in 1999. And this had been partly by chance, as the result of the defection of a Russian agent and the gradual opening of old Kremlin files in the post-Soviet era. When she was exposed, she was living in the same south London house that she had lived in since the 1930s. The press immediately dubbed her 'the spy who came in from the Co-op'.

This exceptional secret agent – who by then was ninety – explained very simply why she had acted as she had. She had looked at the Soviet Union and saw a nation that was striving to give good food and clothes and work and transport to everyone, trying to alleviate poverty and make society more equal. In other words, she had not one regret. She was not prosecuted – in one sense, quite rightly, for what exactly would have been the point by then?

Her story, though, does point to one other aspect of the traitor's life that raises them above the ordinary, and that is the ability to live with the constant fear of being found out. It is easy to imagine the young Melita Norwood, late at night in her darkened office, procuring the blueprints she had seen earlier, and not being certain she was alone in the building as she began the process of photographing them. There must have been paranoia: the pervasive sense of being watched or being followed through the streets. In other words, quite apart from questions of morality, the level of courage shown by this one woman – plus the extraordinary fact that she managed to keep her double life secret until the end of the century – is genuinely remarkable.

Very much less admirable, of course, are the stories of the more privileged but less successful Cambridge Spies. Indeed, there is a sort of mingled squalor and sadness now about these figures that only makes them all the more fascinating. And so it is, incidentally, that some of the puzzles in this section will be inspired by the investigations of MI5 officers such as Arthur Martin, trying to pierce the carapaces of these figures.

It was at Cambridge University in the 1930s that Anthony Blunt, followed by Guy Burgess, Kim Philby, Donald Maclean and John Cairncross, were groomed and recruited. These were bright young men who considered Soviet society to be the future – a future that had to be defended against the rise of fascism. Blunt, Burgess, Philby and Maclean all made their way into the security services during the war: Philby ironically rising to the level where it was his job to seek and root out Russian double agents for MI6. Cairncross, meanwhile, even managed to get a job at Bletchley Park, though it seems scarcely possible that he could have smuggled out the number of vital decrypts that he later claimed without the Park's omniscient internal security having some knowledge of it.

Meanwhile, Guy Burgess and Donald Maclean went on to secure positions as diplomats, again perfectly placed to acquire and pass on confidential material.

In fact, ironically, all of these spies handed over such quantities of material to their Soviet handlers that there was sometimes suspicion in Moscow that they were doubling the double bluff, purveying fake intelligence, loyal to Britain after all.

With the exception of Cairncross, who seemed a scratchy, austere figure, the Cambridge Spies seemed lost in alcohol. Perhaps that

SECRET AGENT BRAINTEASERS

was the only way they could relieve the dreadful pressure of their double lives. Burgess was flamboyant in drink; Maclean became abusively furious; and later on in his life, Blunt was sometimes seen shambling along the London streets, a plastic carrier bag clanking with gin bottles.

But their paranoia about being uncovered was not baseless. Thanks to the previously mentioned post-war decryption coup headed by US and UK codebreakers – codenamed 'Venona' – suspicion first began to fall heavily on Donald Maclean, by now a senior diplomat, and in 1951, he and Guy Burgess defected to the Soviet Union. Thereafter, Kim Philby, who had warned them both that exposure was coming, was under intense suspicion. He denied everything, but was nonetheless forced to resign. In 1963, as the net once more tightened, he too fled the West and crossed the Iron Curtain.

The really intriguing story out of all these desperate tales is the way that Anthony Blunt, who had become director of the Courtauld Institute of Art and an expert in French and Italian painting and architecture, refused to crack. He was interrogated about a dozen times by the MI5 officer Arthur Martin, who was accustomed to success in this sphere, not through any kind of aggression or brutality but instead through native psychological skill. Blunt, by this time knighted, had some form of terrific inner strength. Was it paradoxically his own sense of shame at what he had done that made him defend himself so robustly?

There was another element here too: the royal connection. Blunt had been appointed 'Surveyor of the Queen's Pictures', responsible for curating the extensive art collections to be found in the royal palaces. Blunt could not have been any closer to the centre of the British establishment.

Yet Blunt did crack in the end, in 1964. It was swiftly decided by the authorities first to keep this profound embarrassment an absolute secret and second – in order that this might remain the case – that Blunt should not be prosecuted. And so rather than having to move to Moscow and endure the monotone Soviet life, Blunt simply remained where he was: a member of the best clubs, with access to the finest royal art, and feted by a new generation of young art historians and critics, including Brian Sewell, who were gripped by the depth of his knowledge.

But this life could not last. Blunt was named as a double agent in a book in 1979 and the new Prime Minister Margaret Thatcher could not see why the secrecy had to continue. She named Blunt in the Commons and from that point onwards, the life and identity that he had projected to the world began to dissolve. As well as huge press excitement and uproar, there were the rituals of disgrace, such as the stripping of his knighthood and the loss of royal patronage. Rather movingly, it was his young student Brian Sewell who helped him at this time, giving him accommodation far from the madding press corps.

In the 1988 Alan Bennett play *A Question of Attribution*, there is a mesmerising exchange between Blunt and Her Majesty. They are ostensibly discussing a Titian triptych, the double portrait of a man, and the way that the restoration of the painting appears to be revealing another hidden face beneath. As the conversation goes on, the ambiguities multiply: is Her Majesty really discussing the painting at all?

And here lies the fascination with the traitor as a species: those who suspected Blunt, up to and including the Queen, must have listened to that perfectly languid, plummy voice, absorbed his fascinating and insightful observations about art, and all the time imagined that sensibility having dealings with the chilliest intelligence figures in the Kremlin, betraying a range of national secrets for little, if any, reward. The story of Blunt is in psychological terms the very core of spying, for it is about the apparent impenetrability of the human soul. It was one thing to have been seduced in the 1930s by Soviet sweet talk when little was known of the Stalinist atrocities across Russia and Ukraine: but to persist with that love after the truth about the Soviet regime became known, while at the same time relishing each and every establishment comfort that the British aristocracy and art world could offer?

Today, there are certainly still moles and double agents, at work in every agency across the world. As long as there are secret services, there will be traitors at the heart of them. In fact, these days things might seem even more tangled and confused thanks to Russia's quite brilliant mastery of misdirection, false claims and seeming ideological blankness. The new Cold War seems somehow to lack the chilly certainties of the original.

The puzzles in this section, therefore, are inspired by the never-ending contest of wills between those with something to hide, and those who mean to find them out.

1

CROSS-SECTION

Look at the list of names of diplomats at the negotiating table below. Pair them up so that the combination of the two names makes a word. If their name is on the left they take one view during negotiations, if they are on the right they take the opposing view. Can you work out the tricky diplomacy that is taking place?

ABI	NED
BET	PAT
DES	RAY
ENA	RON
EVE	SID
HAL	TED
LES	TIM
MEL	VIC

2

DOUBLE BLUFF

H	D	I	U	Q	11 S	S	E	G	D	U	5 J
S	13 E	Q	U	A	L	P	R	O	S	E	E
A	X	E	I	R	Y	O	O	D	E	S	T
T	I	I	T	N	U	T	4 S	R	A	K	T
7 S	L	A	E	T	10 S	C	S	E	T	C	Y
W	E	I	N	W	O	L	12 C	V	E	O	N
E	D	S	I	W	1 C	S	A	8 O	D	H	Y
E	O	G	L	H	O	A	R	B	T	14 S	S
P	S	R	E	I	R	G	G	U	I	I	T
L	R	E	K	P	A	A	O	R	L	E	I
A	R	O	O	N	L	9 S	E	H	E	G	U
Y	E	I	6 Y	O	U	N	G	3 S	D	E	2 Q

The words you need to complete the cross-shaped grid contain five letters. They are all hidden in the 12 x 12 letter square. Words go across, backwards, up, down or diagonally. The numbers in the word square correspond to those in the cross-shaped grid – they indicate where the first letter of the answer can be found. When you have discovered your answers in the word square, write them in the grid. But beware! Not everything is what it seems. Can you overcome the double bluff?

3

HUNT OUT THE MOLE

A mole is usually someone who infiltrates an organisation and gains a position of trust over time, making him or her a valuable commodity to an alien group or country.

A word square puzzle reads the same across and down. The words in the list below can make three 4 x 4 word squares each containing the word MOLE. Can you hunt them all out?

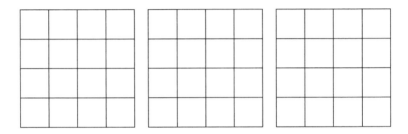

BEEF
COMB
IDOL
IMPS
LUDO
MOLE
MOLE
MOLE
OBOE
PLEA
SEAM
SLIM

4

IN CONVERSATION

The scene is a student common room in the 1930s. Everyone has a glass of sherry in his hand and conversation is flowing freely. An outsider must be identified so you listen to snippets of conversation. Seemingly innocent words are a form of concealment. Who must you not trust?

Barrington: 'We are dealing with danger.'

Caruthers: 'Do not retaliate in haste or anger.'

Grenville: 'A hero seldom receives the rewards he deserves.'

Hildebrand: 'Rations are meagre, yet they are all we have.'

Mortimer: 'So, when will we all meet again?'

Willoughby: 'Do we all agree, nothing must be said?'

5

SAFE HOUSE

In the world of espionage a safe house is used to shelter those who have found themselves in a position of great danger. Make your way to the safe house in the top left-hand corner of the map. To get there, and to avoid suspicion, you must call in at each of the farmhouses on this remote rural route just once. You know the first name of every owner. You cannot retrace your steps. Your first call will be Juanita's house. Who will you ask for when you reach the safety of the safe house?

6

SELECTION PROCESS

Sometimes it's not what is written in a report or appraisal that matters, it's what can be read between the lines. For example, a headmaster's character assessment reading, 'I can confirm this pupil attended my school between the following years . . .' makes it quite clear that some things are best left unsaid!

In a secret file, records are made noting the qualities of the agents. The notes are short, but they are enough to point to which side the agent is on.

Following the pattern, which side will Agent K be on?

Agent A: Depend on her artistic upbringing

Agent B: Fake!

Agent C: Awkward and uncomfortable!

Agent D: An honourable person

Agent E: Night time bearing

Agent F: Invaluable worker, but not a leader

Agent G: Pantomime villain

Agent H: Eyes

Agent I: Disappeared mid-meeting

Agent J: Very correct

7

TAKE TWO

Two-faced, two-timing; where does it all lead? In this crossword there are two clues but only one answer. The solution has two different meanings.

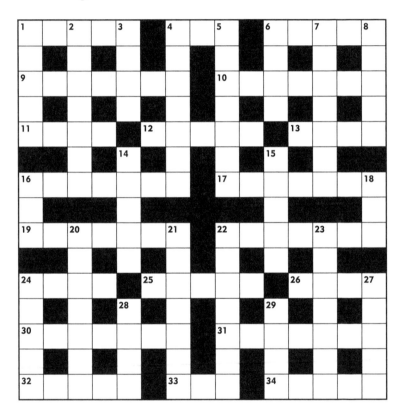

ACROSS

1. Water birds * Quickly bobs out of sight (5)
4. Feather stole * Constricting snake (3)
6. Correct * Not left (5)
9. Affable * Fruit syrup (7)
10. Cupboard * Senior government committee (7)
11. Sketched * Achieved a stalemate (4)
12. Portly * Strong, brown ale (5)
13. Without charge * At liberty (4)
16. Jug * Bowler in baseball (7)
17. Acrobat * Glass beaker (7)
19. Person receiving medical treatment * Tolerant (7)
22. Bird which migrates * Pass food down the throat (7)
24. Colour * Sad (4)
25. Bus * Sports trainer (5)
26. Hyphen * Hurry (4)
30. Take advantage of * Daring adventure (7)
31. Poorly person * Having no legal force (7)
32. Flying toys * Birds of prey (5)
33. Torn piece of cloth * Item of early twentieth century music (3)
34. Paper money * Short messages (5)

DOWN

1. Cubed * Took major risks (5)
2. Happening now * Flow of electricity (7)
3. Stumble * Watery clay to decorate earthenware (4)
4. Large pillow * Strengthen (7)
5. Narrative * Bank facility for depositing and withdrawing money (7)
6. Chest bones * Teases (4)
7. Military officer * Non-specific (7)
8. Heading of a chapter of a book * Name indicating rank or nobility (5)
14. Impudence * Side of the face (5)
15. Daub * Slander (5)
16. Fizzy drink * Burst (3)
18. Propel with an oar * Line (3)
20. Brass instrument * Proclaim loudly (7)
21. Pig's foot * Horse trained to run at a steady pace (7)
22. Hessian * Dismissal (7)
23. Pamphlet * Small piece of foliage (7)
24. Fracture * Short rest from working (5)
27. Conceals * Animal skins (5)
28. Jumps on one leg * Flowers used to make beer (4)
29. Level * A number divisible by two (4)

8

THE THIRD MAN

Kim Philby was dubbed the Third Man following his defection in 1963 after Guy Burgess and Donald Maclean had already done so in 1951. Complete the words below using a man's name of three letters to fill the spaces in each group. Use a different name in each of the sections 1, 2, 3, 4 and 5. Kim is not one of the answers.

1   S _ _ _ A C H
    A _ _ _ I C
    A U _ _ _ A T E D

2   P _ _ _ I S T
    R A D _ _ _ T
    A S _ _ _

3   S O _ _ _ A
    A _ _ _ O M Y
    S E _ _ _ O R

4   S _ _ _ T L E S
    _ _ _ T E N
    S _ _ _ T I S H

5   H _ _ _ W A Y
    B E H _ _ _
    P _ _ _ R E Y

CHAPTER TEN

THE MINISTRY OF SCALLYWAGS

Sometimes in espionage, the simplest mistakes can condemn you to death: automatically looking the wrong way when crossing the road in foreign territory, for instance. For the women and men of the Special Operations Executive (SOE), parachuted in to France, Italy, Greece or Yugoslavia, keeping one's identity secret was a much more complex matter than a simple faked passport and papers. The enemy had eyes everywhere, and anyone whose behaviour stood out even to the most minute degree could face arrest and torture.

There were other rather unique difficulties for these particular special agents, not least of which was remaining blithe and innocent while carrying lethal explosives disguised – according to territory – as anything from lumps of jet-black coal to camel dung. Then there was the forbidden radio equipment: in Europe, transmitters could sometimes come in the guise of exquisitely ornamented antique German clocks. Just as ingenious was the portable transmitter disguised in the middle of a bundle of sticks, which one could put on the back of one's bicycle, while disguised as a rural peasant.

So the puzzles in this section pay tribute in part to the wartime department that was instructed by Winston Churchill to 'set Europe ablaze' and also to its domestic equivalent, the secret trained guerrillas known as 'the Scallywags', whose job was to mount bloody resistance to any possible Nazi invasion. As well as some practical tests, of the type thrown at budding recruits to the SOE, this chapter also includes lateral-thinking timed puzzles to do with sending vital messages from hidden locations as the enemy is closing in; puzzles inspired by some of the more extraordinary gadgetry that was devised in the laboratories of one Colonel Gubbins (of whom more later); and encryption puzzles inspired by the work of Leo Marks, an SOE figure who devised clever code-passing techniques involving squares of silk. From the start, the SOE was different to the broader department of MI6 in one main respect. While MI6 was about spying to gather intelligence, the SOE was espionage in the cause of sabotage and subversion. The job of its agents involved blowing up railway lines and power stations, as well as making contact with local rebels, helping to arm and organise them. If MI6 agents were the smooth operators, the SOE spies were almost anarchic in their dedication to destructive action.

As a department, it recruited from a broad section of women and men. Perhaps the most famous now is Violette Szabo, née Bushell, born of a French mother and English father in Paris and brought up in London. She worked in a department store in Brixton at the perfume counter. When her husband Étienne was killed during the battle of El-Alamein in 1942, she decided to join up with the Auxiliary Territorial Service.

To put this into some context, it's worth noting she had only recently given birth to a daughter, Tania. Violette's compulsion to take a more active role in the war against the Nazis was the beginning of a quite extraordinary story of sacrifice and bravery; in part, it was the story of a mother fighting for the future of her child.

It was while she was in the ATS that raptor-eyed recruiters spotted her potential and she was approached to join the SOE French section. Her ease and fluency with the language on all levels was an invaluable asset. But they needed more than a linguist: they wanted someone who could be dropped into France in order to help and strengthen the Resistance.

Training for the SOE took place in several secret locations: country estates in the New Forest, Hampshire, and up in the Highlands of Scotland. It was gruelling. There were assault courses in forests, marches over mountains, night navigation and map reading. That was just the start – the establishment of physical fitness. What followed was a crash course in ruthlessness. There was weapons training: gun proficiency (she had a head start as her father had taught her to shoot) and also combat with knives. Recruits were taught how to kill silently and cold-bloodedly in both armed and unarmed, hand-to-hand combat. Other branches of espionage might have had moments of amused escapism; by contrast, this initiation would have told recruits just how chillingly, terribly serious their missions would be.

Together with their fresh killing skills, the recruits were also taught the core dark arts that would be at the heart of their work: where best on railway lines to set explosives to cause maximum damage; where to set the charges on the walls of factories and power plants to bring the entire building crashing down. Added to all this, recruits had to become proficient in Morse code. Radios would be central to their work. Indeed, in some of the wild, inhospitable territories in which they would soon be finding themselves, the radio would be the sole lifeline to friends. Then there were courses on lock-picking; there was a method involving a protractor that the instructors swore by.

Violette Szabo signed up for all of this, along with several other recruits drawn from many unexpected quarters, including the internment camps on the Isle of Man for Italian citizens.

Perhaps the element of training that might have most underlined the fearsome danger of all that lay ahead was the parachute jumping. Agents had to learn to carry with them a small shovel, so that when they landed they could immediately bury any trace of the parachute. On one of these practice jumps, Violette Szabo hurt her leg, yet still she persisted.

It must have taken some extraordinary strength of will not to dwell on the obvious. What if she was parachuted into enemy territory and was immediately injured in the same way? This is to say nothing of the speculation about a hundred other hideous hazards.

Yet she must also have known just how important the SOE and its work was. Her superiors may have told her of earlier triumphs involving the complete destruction of a French power station, the spectacular demolition of a railway bridge in Nazi-occupied Greece – and indeed the assassination of one of the chief architects of the

Holocaust, Reinhard Heydrich, blown up in his car and his flesh in part shredded by the thousands of horse-hairs which had been in the seat upholstery.

Whatever her motivations, Violette's first mission was in April 1944: she was parachuted into France. Her cover story was that she was a travelling saleswoman. Her mission was to make contact with a Resistance figure called Philippe Liewer, investigate the disappearance of other SOE agents in Rouen, carry out local acts of sabotage, and to monitor any industrial work that the Germans were carrying out in the area.

She was armed with a code poem which is now very famous. It began: 'The life that I have / Is all that I have / And the life that I have is yours'. It was written by SOE genius Leo Marks; these and other compositions were used to conceal hidden messages (though it is now not clear precisely what lay within this one).

After a few weeks out in the field, evading suspicion because of her perfectly French sensibilities and manner, Violette Szabo was able to return to Britain. Just one day after the Allied forces stormed the beaches of Normandy, she was once more flown back into France, as part of the general assault on the entire Nazi war infrastructure. She was paired up with a Resistance agent known as 'Anastasie'. Then one afternoon, as they were driving through the countryside, the car loaded with bicycles and weapons, they accidentally hit a German road block.

Anastasie told Violette to run; instead, she reached for the gun. A furious exchange of bullets ensued. The two agents jumped out of the car, dived into a wheat field – but Violette did not get away. There was a suggestion that it was Violette's earlier ankle injury that prevented her sprinting for it. But there was also a rather more heroic explanation for her action: as the German soldiers approached her hiding place in the wheat, she was allowing Anastasie to escape unnoticed.

She was said to have laughed when the soldiers asked her where her companion was. The soldiers took her into custody, where she faced a nightmare of brutal interrogation. But she refused to give her captors the intelligence they wanted, so she was transported to

Ravensbrück concentration camp. After being subjected to starvation, further assaults, and physically debilitating forced labour, the terribly weakened Szabo faced execution. She was shot in the back of the head. She was only twenty-three.

A little after the war, her little girl Tania was present at the posthumous ceremony to award her mother the George Cross. To this day, it remains the most remarkable story of courage in espionage.

It is also a fascinating window into the way that mental resourcefulness was deployed in the SOE. Operatives had to both obtain intelligence and use it ruthlessly against the enemy. It was the SOE who could claim credit for blowing up a 'heavy water' facility in Norway – an industrial installation that was being used to help develop Nazi atomic weaponry. These were actions that sometimes had a more profound effect than the rival service MI6 might ever have cared to admit.

That said, even the gravest of the agents in this department must occasionally have allowed themselves an amused raised eyebrow at some of the ingenious ideas that flashed through SOE's headquarters in Baker Street. The aforementioned Colonel Gubbins devised all manner of extraordinary gimmicks. There were guns made to look like pens and briefcases containing hidden daggers. Radio aerials were fashioned to look like organic tendrils, which would blend in perfectly when hanging among the branches of a tree; briefcases were rigged with potassium nitrate inside, so that if one was apprehended with vital documents, papers would be burnt before the enemy could even get the case open.

If you wanted a means of disabling an enemy vehicle, in order to get a head start, or rendering enemy binoculars useless to help evade capture, then the answer was 'face cream'. This was a substance that came in a cosmetics tube that – when applied to windscreens or any kind of glass – would frost it within minutes.

There were explosive fuses shaped like pencils. There were disguise kits involving toupees and false teeth (how the original 'C', Mansfield Cumming, a great disguise enthusiast, would have loved the techniques for subtly changing the shape of the jaw, or altering the shape of the face with well-chosen spectacles). There were even matchboxes and cigarette cartons that came with fake labels to be stuck on in the appropriate territory, with false bottoms for the concealment of tiny items.

And then there were the bombs. It was not just faked camel dung that could conceal explosives. Other means included incendiary soap – when it came into contact with water, the moisture would seep through the soap to the pure metallic sodium concealed at its centre and burn fiercely. There were also lethal tins of soup, planted in the larders of deserted houses and designed to go off after they had been looted and then opened by enemy soldiers.

Meanwhile, as the Special Operations Executive went about its inflammatory business in Europe, there was a secret department back in Britain that was poised to spring into lethal action should ever the Germans get a toehold on British soil. This was the department of Scallywags: the nickname given to around 6,000 volunteers who had been trained to become potentially lethal assassins, as well as knowing all the destructive rudiments of sabotage.

These volunteers sometimes were men either slightly too old or slightly too young to be drawn into the army. Some were in the Home Guard, some were in reserved occupations, and others were clergymen, dentists and gamekeepers. It is rumoured that among their number was a young firebrand journalist, rather short-sighted, who would go on to become leader of the Labour Party. His name was Michael Foot. All volunteers were a very far cry from *Dad's Army*'s Captain Mainwaring. Like their SOE counterparts, they had been tutored in the arts of ruthless espionage.

The men were effectively sleeper agents, in the sense that they would only be activated once warning church bells had rung out with the news of the invasion of British soil. In this eventuality, they had their confidential instructions: to make their way to secret bases dotted all around the country, and obtain the weapons and explosive equipment that had been stashed in them.

As soon as the German soldiers materialised, these otherwise unremarkable-seeming figures would set about a programme of maximum disruption, to be carried out at night: destroying key railway lines, lorry parks, certain telephone wires. Because they were civilians, capture by the Germans would have meant not imprisonment but execution.

The official, if still secret, name for this group (the members of which did not know each other outside of local units of eight or nine operatives) was the Auxiliers. They all had revolvers. In the early days of the war, they were encouraged to carry out training exercises at night. This could lead to awkward encounters with vigilant policemen on night watch. Some Scallywags found themselves taken into the station and locked in cells under suspicion of being enemy spies, but all the Auxiliers carried cards with a telephone number on it in case of such circumstances. Police trying the number found that it was for a Whitehall department, and that their suspects were engaged in secret work for the government.

Because of the intensely undercover nature both of identities and of the very notion of the Scallywags, the Auxiliers in question never received any official post-war gratitude. And indeed it was only a few years back that scanty details began to be released into the archives.

One man who had volunteered recalled, decades later, that among the equipment and instructions was a jar of brandy. The seal on it was to be opened if capture by Nazis seemed imminent. It was thought that a few glugs would boost morale and enable them to withstand interrogation for longer. It would also serve – in an emergency involving an injury, say – as a makeshift anaesthetic. The Scallywags were apparently displeased at the end of the war when – in true Civil Service form-ticking style – they were instructed to return the jars of brandy because they counted as equipment. And indeed the jars were sent back: but in many cases the brandy had been drunk and they were returned with an altogether different liquid inside!

So the puzzles that follow also feature that theme of mavericks on missions. In amid the astonishing courage and determination of the SOE agents, there is also a brilliant and unselfconscious quirkiness, plus also a sense of anti-establishment fearlessness. To fight alongside comrades is one thing: to be an individual agent spirited into a strange land, where even the remotest mountain shepherds might be acting as eyes and ears to the enemy, goes right to the heart of the extraordinary reserves of self-sufficiency and level-headed coolness that any operative needs.

1

BIRD'S-EYE VIEW

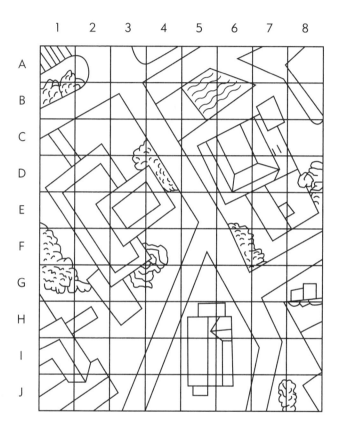

A reconnaissance mission involves flying over a hostile airfield. The bird's-eye view shows a plan of the area. The enlarged square denotes the precise location for a parachute drop. Unhelpfully, the square may or may not be the same way round as the areas in the sketch. All the same, there is only one squared area that correlates.

Can you locate the place for the parachutist to land?

2

CAREFUL CONCEALMENT

In order to safeguard the agent in the field, new clothing was supplied, correct to the smallest detail, so that the disguise was foolproof.

Reveal the items of clothing issued to agents in World War II by completing the three-letter words reading down in each section.

1 W W P I J A

   — — — — — —

   Y T Y P T E

2 A O T I V U

   — — — — — —

   E D E Y X E

3 A J T A F E E I

   — — — — — — — —

   T Y Y D R G R K

4 S B S A C E P A

   — — — — — — — —

   A Y Y E W E W M

5 C R M A A H J S

   — — — — — — — —

   Y M X T E P B Y

3

DISGUISED

S	T	U	N	T	E	D
B	E	D	R	O	O	M
N	O	U	G	H	T	S
T	E	A	C	H	E	R
H	O	R	M	O	N	E
T	O	P	S	I	D	E
P	A	R	S	L	E	Y

Those involved in the Special Operations Executive and the Ministry of Scallywags were masters (or mistresses) of disguise. The words in the upper grid are all in disguise: they are anagrams of other words. Once you have solved the anagrams, write them in the lower grid (in the same order) to reveal a word in the central column that gives a vital message.

4

FOOD FOR THOUGHT

L	A	W	S	S	F	O	V	I	E	W
U	A	A	C	R	O	B	A	T	K	A
T	U	N	A	T	X	H	G	E	A	R
E	N	T	R	Y	I	B	U	M	P	Y
S	K	P	F	A	B	L	E	A	P	P
K	E	Y	E	C	R	I	A	F	L	Y
N	M	D	C	H	E	S	T	E	A	A
S	P	R	A	T	T	S	H	R	U	B
E	T	O	N	A	J	T	R	O	D	E
N	O	P	A	R	A	S	O	L	N	A
D	U	E	L	C	R	E	W	E	A	K

In the grid opposite there are no black squares, as you might find in a traditional crossword. Extra letters have taken the place of black squares. We give you the ACROSS and DOWN clues but do not reveal where they fit in the grid. All answers contain either three, four, five or seven letters. When you have solved all the clues and pinpointed their location, the unused letters will spell out a message. This tells the recipient what to do once the message has been read. We suggest you do not do this!

ACROSS

1. Legal rules
5. Opinion
8. Gymnastic performer
9. Food fish
11. Apparatus or equipment
13. Record logged in a diary
15. Uneven, regarding a road or field
16. Story with a meaning
17. Unlocking instrument
18. Insect
19. Coffer
21. Small herring
23. Bush
26. School near Windsor
28. Travelled on horseback
29. Sunshade
30. Deadly contest for two
31. Feeble

DOWN

1. Stringed instrument
2. Need
3. Square worn around the neck
4. Cunning creature
5. Indistinct
6. Thing
7. Cautious
10. Scruffy
12. Clap
14. Sailing boat
15. Perfect joy
19. Manmade waterway
20. Hurl
21. Despatch
22. Cord
24. Part in a play
25. Bird's jaw
27. Glass container

5

ON TRACK

Some operatives have discovered that there is valuable cargo stored in the two train coaches locked away in a goods yard. Coach 1 contains weapons that are bound for an army barracks. Coach 2 contains paintings and sculpture bound for an exhibition at a museum. Next day, both coaches will be picked up and moved on to their different destinations. Apart from some signs that are relatively easy to transfer, the two coaches look exactly alike.

Wouldn't it be a great jaunt to switch the carriages round? Think of the chaos that will be caused when it comes to unloading!

Pictured opposite is a plan of the goods yard. The area is fenced and it is not possible to take the engine out on to the main line.

The train coaches can only be moved by being coupled with the engine and being either pushed or pulled along the railtrack. The most easterly section of track has a weight restriction. It can take the weight of the engine, but NOT the weight of any of the carriages.

Can the two coaches be swapped over with the engine returned to its original position, just as if nothing had happened?

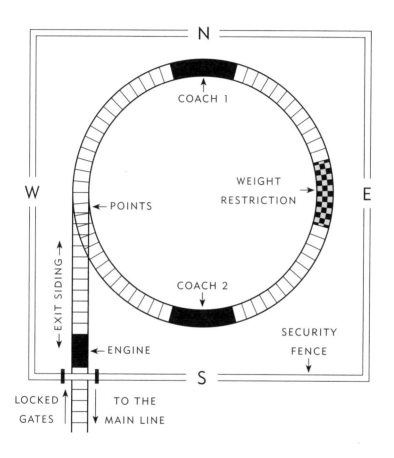

6

SOMETHING TO HIDE

Sometimes it's what you don't see rather than what you do.

Look at each group of words below. In each case a letter can be added to the front of the words in the group to make another. Rearrange these letters to make the name of a famous and distinctive wine. Its bottles made a cunning and careful hiding place for something that had to remain hidden.

1 HILL   HOP   OAT   RESTED

2 GAIN   GENT   HEAD   MAZE

3 CONIC   RATE   RON   VAN

4 HATCH   RAIN   ROUBLE   WIGS

5 EATING   EDGES   ERRING   OWL

6 AILED   ARROW   EAR   ICE

7 DEAL   ON   RAN   RISES

THE MINISTRY OF SCALLYWAGS

7

SPECIAL DELIVERY

You are waiting for a special delivery. You receive the five separate messages below about a series of top-secret consignments. At first the messages seem to have no link and no apparent meaning. However, that is far from the truth. After some careful thought, what can you construe from the messages?

1   At the last minute Monica rearranged all her appointments.

2   I will take the risk if future success of the mission is at stake.

3   The group untied the rope before moving on downstream.

4   There are grey clouds overhead, but will it rain, I wonder?

5   A little of what you fancy clearly does you good.

8

TINNED FOODS

Tinned foods were carried as essential rations wherever the action was taking place. Sometimes the metal containers had an even more sinister purpose as they were used to conceal explosives or weapons. In this puzzle, two items of food are concealed in each line of letters by shuffling the letters. In each individual group the two words are the same length, and the letters remain in the correct sequence.

1 B M I R O T N C H E

2 M A P E A N C G O H

3 K S A I L P M P O E R N

4 C D A H M E S R O R N Y

5 A S A N C R H D O I N V E Y

CHAPTER ELEVEN

THE THRILLING DENOUEMENT

There are those who might think that the future of spying lies wholly in computer algorithms. They are wrong. Espionage will always need 'the human factor' (the title used by Graham Greene for his 1978 spy novel). And despite the unthinkable advances in surveillance technology, making it possible to track an agent on every continent, there are some elements of undercover work that have remained the same throughout history, and which will continue as long as there are competing nations and civilisations.

No machine can yet replicate a devious cast of mind; no artificial intelligence can dissemble convincingly. Nor can there be a computerised replication of the most fundamental emotions that make spying successful: susceptibility to flattery, divided loyalties, simple sexual attraction, frustration, anger, fear. The greatest skill of the spy is to play upon the human passions of those with the required information, and make those passions resonate to one's own purposes.

In addition to this is the fuel that marks the most brilliant feats of espionage: adrenaline. Whether it is getting across an enemy border having stolen the required information or holding your nerve as the enemy begins to suspect your true identity, the agents concerned must find a way of using that pulsing heart rate and nauseous anxiety to the fullest effect.

To this end, the puzzles in this section raise the stakes: from working out the correct way to pick the lock to escape the enemy compound, to finding the correct code that will stop the bomb timer, to encrypting the vital message to be transmitted that will prevent two aggressive nations going to war, these will be tests of sharp common sense balanced against tough time limits.

It is certainly true that if we glance across the entire history of espionage, we will see that the greatest and most notable practitioners of this art would have understood very well this key ability to keep the thoughts sharp in moments of intense pressure.

The eighteenth-century Venetian eroticist Giacomo Casanova was, for a time, a spy in France, working at the behest of Parisian noblemen: if he were with us today, any number of intelligence services would be queuing to use him. Casanova, a formidable polymath who could turn his hand from literature to medicine to diplomacy, had travelled extensively and met some of the towering figures of the age, from Frederick the Great of Prussia to Catherine the Great of Russia. This elegant man, the son of actors, was an intense sensualist: his life spent in pursuit not merely of women, but of the finest food, art, clothing, perfumes. His innate talent for seduction would have been perfect for espionage and he was also very sharp on some of the other, darker skills required.

At one point, he was thrown into prison in Venice by the city's ruling Council of Ten, in the dungeons located near the state rooms of the Doge's Palace. Escape would have seemed impossible – none had ever managed it. Yet Casanova had patience and cunning, and with the help of a fellow prisoner, Father Balbi, he managed to get hold of a length of metal and concealed it in his cell chair. Painstakingly, over weeks, he sharpened the metal, and then used it to slowly chisel a hole through the wooden boards of the cell. He made his eventual breathtaking escape via the roof, then lowered himself into the public space of the Doge's courtyard, from which he then vanished into the ghostly labyrinth of Venice. He rematerialised in Paris, beyond the clutches of his captors.

Another figure from the darkened past who would take the most intense interest in the modern workings of MI5 and MI6 is Francis Walsingham, the late sixteenth-century spymaster in the court of Elizabeth I. He was the Tudor equivalent of 'C' or 'M', but unlike those figures, there was nothing genial or benevolent about him. He ran a network of secret agents and, as a firm Protestant, was utterly ruthless about suppressing Catholic conspiracies. His spies were young, ambitious men drawn from Oxford and Cambridge universities. Some would find themselves posted abroad to Catholic Europe to infiltrate and report back all intelligence concerning Elizabeth and her throne.

This was a dark world of violence and torture; there are theories that the young playwright Christopher Marlowe, stabbed through the eye in an apparent drunken fight in Deptford, was a Catholic double agent, working for the Crown but connected with continental contacts feverish to bring down the Protestant Queen.

Above all, Walsingham pulsed with hatred and fear for Elizabeth's Catholic cousin Mary Queen of Scots, and the influence that she had. Patiently – and quite without any kind of pity – he devised a trap for herself and her eager young Catholic followers. This became known as the Babington Plot, named after one of those followers, Anthony Babington, and it involved coded messages being smuggled in beer barrels from Mary to her allies. Walsingham, having tricked all parties via a double agent into initiating this means of communication, was able to intercept and decode every line of every letter.

It was not long before Anthony Babington in his enthusiasm began voicing treachery in these letters, and when he in turn received a letter purporting to be from Mary, with a forged signature, he and his companions were tricked into committing to paper the names of all those in on their plans. Now was the time for Walsingham to strike: the young Catholics were hanged, then cut down while still alive, disembowelled and castrated. Mary Queen of Scots faced decapitation; it is said that her executioner was so nervous that his aim was affected. Horrifically, neither the first nor the second blow of the axe did the job, and her head only came off with the third.

Before the sentence was carried out, Mary bitterly denounced Walsingham, and his plots for her 'destruction'. He calmly replied: 'I have done nothing unworthy of an honest man.' Then – as now – for any senior officer or spymaster, their loyalties and convictions must be so absolute that the words of their opponents cannot begin to scratch at these certainties. Yet coupled with this iron will must also be the subterranean knowledge that their own lives may be sharply ended, in pain and terror.

In much more recent times, there has been one spymaster whose extraordinary bravery matches any fictional or cinematic secret agent: indeed, this figure's escape across the border was many times more dramatic than the climax of Ian Fleming's *From Russia with Love* and his intelligence was instrumental in saving both America and Russia from mistakenly raining down nuclear missiles upon each other's nations. Oleg Gordievsky's story, in fact, is perhaps the quintessential espionage fable: a blend of high conscience and principles at a time in the Cold War when the slightest false move on either side could ignite a conflict that would leave whole cities as flattened irradiated deserts.

Gordievsky, born in Moscow in 1938, was trained by the NKVD, forerunners of the KGB, and as a young agent, he was posted to East Berlin. As he grew in experience, so postings to other countries in the guise of a diplomat followed. Yet his superiors were unaware that Gordievsky's views on the legitimacy of Soviet rule were sharply affected in 1968 by the 'Prague Spring'. This was the period in which Prime Minister Alexandr Dubček's move to liberalise Czech society – removing state controls over industry, free media, more fluid travel – led to the rise of opposition parties and the looming possibility that the country might reject communism altogether. The response from Moscow was heavy: around 650,000 troops were sent to Czechoslovakia, the streets were filled with tanks, and Dubček was removed from power. Soviet leader Leonid Brezhnev would not countenance any country in the Soviet bloc pulling away from its influence. But agent Gordievsky was repelled by the oppression.

It was while he was stationed in Denmark that – through intermediaries – Gordievsky made contact with MI6. From the early 1970s, he began to provide them with intelligence.

In 1982, Gordievsky was posted to London, to be a 'diplomat' in the Russian embassy in Kensington; he was now the most perfectly placed double agent. In fact, in the light of recently released confidential papers, it appears that he was extremely influential in the super-powers pulling back from the nuclear brink. In 1983, geopolitical tension was infernal: President Reagan had labelled the Soviet Union 'the Evil Empire', the Soviets had mistakenly shot a Korean passenger jet out of the sky, and in the autumn, the western forces of NATO began a vast training exercise codenamed 'Operation Able Archer' which was based on a hypothetical Soviet grab for European territory. This exercise would involve everything from fighter jets to submarines in the Barents Sea.

The aged Soviet leader Yuri Andropov and those around him in the Kremlin were convinced, however, that it was an elaborate trick. They believed that such an exercise was actually a cover for a genuine attack by America on Russia. Accordingly, every Soviet nuclear warhead was primed in readiness for counter-attack. The misinterpretation of any element of 'Operation Able Archer' could have led to the button being pushed. This was the closest that the world had come to all-out atomic holocaust since the Cuban Crisis of 1962.

It was Gordievsky who secretly let Margaret Thatcher know, via MI6, just exactly how paranoid the Soviet leadership was, and just what sort of an effect these NATO training exercises were having. Gordievsky briefed the government on the depth of Kremlin bunker mentality, and on the genuine fear felt by these old men of the Soviet regime.

He was also the first to inform Mrs Thatcher, again through MI6, of a younger Kremlin figure, a rising star called Mikhail Gorbachev, whose approach was more pragmatic. This intelligence was instrumental in persuading Mrs Thatcher and Ronald Reagan into toning down the public belligerence. From that point, the approach was more cautious and exploratory.

But a crisis loomed for Oleg Gordievsky: in 1985, he was recalled from London to Moscow. And it was there, one day, that he was taken deep into KGB headquarters and interrogated with truth drugs. It was possible that he had been betrayed by an American double agent. Extraordinarily, he managed to maintain his own cover story under the onslaught of questioning, and he was released. But it was clear that the suspicions were growing, and that the next time he was pulled in, there would be no compunction about taking him to the basement to be shot in the back of the head.

What followed was the most astounding series of spy versus spy manoeuvres. MI6 had deep cover agents in Moscow; while out on a jog, Gordievsky passed one such agent and quickly indicated via a facial expression his sense of alarm at the situation he was in. This was all MI6 needed by means of confirmation.

Gordievsky was sent a hardback edition of Shakespeare's sonnets. By moistening the flyleaf paper, he was able to draw the layers apart to reveal a thin cellophane square within. Upon this was written his escape instructions.

Another jog, this time managing to get away from the ubiquitous surveillance of the KGB. Now he was at a railway station and then on a train taking him close to the border with Finland. As he got off the train, he was met by two MI6 agents, one man and a woman with a baby. Gordievsky now had to face the claustrophobia of a car boot. The idea was to drive him, concealed, across the Russian border to Finland. However, he and his agent friends had to negotiate ruthlessly policed border posts. Discovery would have been disastrous for all, and deadly for him.

At the first post, Gordievsky had to wrap himself in a silver blanket; this was to evade the primitive thermal imaging detectors that guards were employing. But at the second post, even more tightly policed, with watchtowers and barbed wire, the guards were more scrupulous. Gordievsky, crammed in the boot, listened as he heard the sound of frantic sniffing. They were using dogs.

It was at this point that the female agent got out of the car with her baby and announced that it badly needed changing. She put the infant on the bonnet of the boot, with a blanket, and proceeded to change its nappy. She then dropped the old one to the ground. This fresh scent threw the dogs off.

Gordievsky and his friends successfully crossed over to Finland, and from that point, sanctuary loomed. Even more gratifyingly, a few months afterwards, now relocated to London, the agent was reunited with his family, who had been in Azerbaijan when he had defected. And by the autumn of that year, Russia had a new premier. Mikhail Gorbachev, it transpired, was indeed eager to make changes and to do business with western powers. Most unusually for a real-life spy story, Gordievsky won warm praise from deep within the British establishment, eventually being honoured. It is not often that double agents get to enjoy peaceful and praise-filled retirements. This one, however, was more than earned: his story illustrates perfectly the fact that for all the murkiness and the shadows, spying can in fact frequently be a higher moral calling, a chance even to fight for peace. However, it might also be the case that a few old colleagues from his KGB days may not have taken such a sunny view of his career.

And so this final tranche of puzzles represents the sweaty denouement: the quick-thinking solution to evade granite-faced border guards, the Elizabethan codes that will prevent the assassination of the Queen, an eighteenth-century Venetian jail puzzle, as Casanova strives to escape the Council of Ten. The principles, no matter the period setting, are all the same: here is a crisis. And in some cases, not only is your life at stake, but the lives of many others. Against pitiless time limits, can you crack the conundrums and keep your cool?

1

BEAT THE CLOCK

The clock is ticking and time is running out as an explosive device has been triggered. The control can be overridden by turning the dial . . . but in which direction? Do you go clockwise or anticlockwise?

Solve the clues opposite and fit the eight-letter answers into the correct places in the grid. The first letter of every answer appears in a numbered area. The answers go round in a circle and may fit in clockwise or anticlockwise – it is up to you to work this out. Which are there more of, clockwise or anticlockwise answers? Turn the dial in the direction corresponding with the greatest total and diffuse the danger!

1. International travel document
2. Location, often rural, where planes take off and land
3. Foolishly oblivious to danger
4. Member of a military unit who carried out raids in enemy territory
5. Information from a document, which supports a fact or proposition
6. Metal restraint attached to the wrist
7. Outbreak of unpremeditated fighting of a small group
8. Carried out a surprise attack from a concealed position
9. Work one's way into another's affections
10. Eavesdrop, listen unintentionally
11. Person who is on the run
12. Make a tentative proposal
13. Alter one's appearance to conceal identity
14. Stella Rimington became _____ General of MI5
15. Intersection of roads or rivers
16. Person unknown
17. Deliberate damage or destruction
18. Hired killer
19. Explosive device, programmed to explode at a precise moment (4.4)
20. Teaching or learning a specific skill or discipline
21. Picks up or fetches an item or items
22. Very thin dagger
23. Official working in an embassy overseas
24. The act of putting an individual or country in the hands of the enemy
25. Strategic plan or timetable
26. Broadcast, pass a message over the airwaves
27. Individual who pretends to be someone else
28. Sentence worded to request information

2

DIGITAL DEVICES

Messages with numbers, but how important are they? Can you calculate their significance?

1 505 31773 51 771

2 337 5335 7105

3 317704 57735 53045

4 345 51 5107 7714

5 31573 53507 5537

3

DIPLOMACY

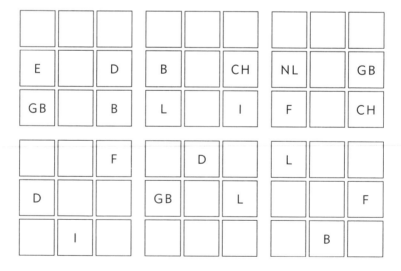

	D						F	
NL			CH	D				B
		E		L		CH		

Sometimes the only way to sort out a problem is to assemble all the relevant nations around a conference table and get them to talk to each other. Diplomacy is key here. Protocol must be respected as you allocate places in the conference hall for the nine countries attending the summit meeting. Each country has nine delegates each represented by the international registration plates of their motor vehicles. Fill the grid with the registration plates so that each block of 3 x 3 squares contains all nine different plates as does each of the nine rows reading across and the nine columns reading down.

Belgium is represented by B.

France is represented by F.

Germany is represented by D.

Great Britain is represented by GB.

Italy is represented by I.

Luxembourg is represented by L.

Netherlands is represented by NL.

Spain is represented by E.

Switzerland is represented by CH.

4

COUNTDOWN

Much of the work carried out by the secret services can be slow and painstaking. In this section, however, speed is key. The clock is ticking but how quickly can you come up with the solutions to these quickfire mental manoeuvres?

1 Burgess and Maclean defected in 1951. Philby defected in 1963. Blunt was exposed in 1979. How many days were there in those three years?

2 What number do you get if you add up all the individual digits in those three years?

3 Multiply the number of reigning British monarchs in the first half of the twentieth century, by the number of reigning British monarchs in the second half of the twentieth century, and multiply that by the number of letters in Buckingham Palace.

4 Which is worth more at face value, 144 decimal 10p pieces or 120 pre decimal half crowns?

5 Which is the greater number, the number of seconds in a week, or the number of feet in 100 miles?

5

ELIZABETHAN ESPIONAGE

THE MESSAGE

Francis Walsingham is widely considered to be one of the first ever spymasters. Working in the reign of Elizabeth I, he was busy in an era of court intrigue where nobody's safety could be guaranteed, least of all that of the monarch herself.

This message has been delivered by one of the court musicians and must be decoded as a matter of urgency. The beginning and end points of a decoding pattern are available; you know the combination of two symbols that makes up the letters A plus Y/Z but what about the other letters? Can you work out the message?

6

EXPLOSIVE ELEMENTS

Not all operatives had a so-called desk job. Many worked out in the field. The words in the puzzles below have been blown apart in an act of sabotage. The words in the left-hand columns remain in the correct order, but the words in the right-hand columns have been scattered. A single letter can be added to the end of the first column, which then becomes the first letter of the next word. Plurals are not allowed. When you have put everything back together, what message is revealed reading down? There are two words to find. The first word is found from the two columns 1–6. The second word is found from the two columns 7–12.

Words for left-hand column numbers 1 to 6: FAR, EON, ACE, OAT, RUM, CRU

1　FUN　—　＿ ＿ ＿　FAR

2　ARE　—　＿ ＿ ＿　EON

3　LAW　—　＿ ＿ ＿　ACE

4　FAN　—　＿ ＿ ＿　OAT

5　WOK　—　＿ ＿ ＿　RUM

6　SPA　—　＿ ＿ ＿　CRU

Words for right-hand column numbers 7 to 12: SPY, RAT, USE, OUR, EAT, BUT

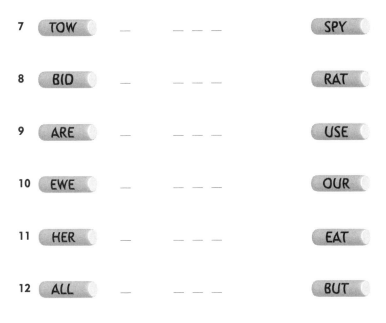

7   TOW   —   _ _ _   SPY

8   BID   —   _ _ _   RAT

9   ARE   —   _ _ _   USE

10 EWE   —   _ _ _   OUR

11 HER   —   _ _ _   EAT

12 ALL   —   _ _ _   BUT

7

FLAT NUMBER

You were expecting to be given the number of an apartment where a secret meeting was to take place.

Instead you receive a note showing two sums.

Can you crack the code and find the flat?

ERA +
EAR
——
ARE

A + E × R = FLAT NUMBER

8

I-SPY

All the twenty listed words must be fitted back into the grid. Words can go either across or down.

While speed is always of the essence, it is important to keep cool. There are many ways to nearly solve this challenge. There's only one way to complete it!

EAT	ERR	EYE	ILL	OAR
RUG	SAP	SAT	SEW	SLY
SPY	TAG	TIP	TOW	USE
YEN	YES	YET	YEW	WIN

9

IMPOSTORS

Six words, each with a choice of definitions. Can you match the words with their definitions and weed out all the impostors?

1 HIPPOLOGY
  a) the study of the 1960s
  b) the study of horses
  c) the study of bones

2 ZORILLA
  a) an African mammal of the weasel family
  b) an expert sword fighter
  c) a Mexican bugle

3 POTSHERD
  a) a feeding trough
  b) a tray for holding dried flower petals
  c) a piece of broken ceramic material

4 QUATORZAIN
  a) a fourteen line poem
  b) a fourteen day holiday
  c) a four-pronged pikestaff

5 JIGGER
  a) a leather strap used in falconry
  b) a tropical flea
  c) a Malaysian flat-bottomed boat

6 IMPOST
  a) a tax or duty
  b) the upper part of a pillar carrying an arch
  c) the weight carried by a horse in a handicap race

10

MOVING ON

Moving one letter at a time, change the top word into the bottom one in both examples. A new word must be formed at every step.

The fifth word in the first list and the third word in the second list will tell you how you are moving on.

M A J O R

— — — — —

— — — — —

— — — — —

— — — — —

L I N E N

S L A N T

— — — — —

— — — — —

— — — — —

— — — — —

P E N C E

11

OUT OF ORDER

The telephones are out of order yet important information must get through. The telephonist can communicate which number on the rotary dial would be used, but is not able to give the exact letter, which means there is a choice of which is correct, e.g. if 2 is dialled it could be either A, B or C. Using the numbers below, can you work out the information?

1   255/88284668/23/77372733/367/228466

2   843/06864/626/428/2768833/843/267337/46/34848483

3   5337/2/5665688/367/48273/3648

     8430/273/326437688

12

VENETIAN VENTURE

A daredevil such as Casanova would have been familiar with the labyrinth of secret tunnels and disguised doors in the splendid and palatial buildings of Venice. There is a section on the top row of this wall of tiles that will open a concealed door – a handy means of exit in a crisis situation. There is a set sequence of events to activate the mechanism. One certain tile on each row needs to be pushed, starting somewhere on the bottom row and working up to the top. You can only move upward each time, to a tile directly above, or diagonally to the immediate left or right above. There is a logical route to take.

Which tile on the top row completes the move and opens the secret door?

START

CONCLUSION

The technology becomes ever more astoundingly (and sometimes amusingly) inventive: there are, for instance, contact lenses you can wear that can take pictures of people under surveillance and transmit them with a simple double-blink. Those of a certain age may recall the time when microdots were considered the outer edge of sci-fi spy cool. But the principle remains exactly the same: nation states will never lose their appetite for the secrets of others. And they will never stop devising the means to grab them.

Possibly the one change that might be ascribed to MI5 and MI6 these days is not only that they have stepped out from the shadows, but that these agencies have also been so thoroughly professionalised. There is no longer the sense that they are autonomous and therefore in some way above normal laws. They have become – in a way that curiously they were not before – respectable.

Today's spy is not (by and large) a haunted existentialist cynic; she is instead somewhere between a businesswoman and a brisk military officer. Espionage still requires the greatest guile and in some cases exceptional courage, but that sense of standing slightly outside of everyday society has receded. The spies have come in from the cold and are advertising in friendly tones for recruits in the *Guardian*.

There will never be any shortage of applicants; nor indeed will the taps on the shoulder ever cease. Today, the approach might just as easily go to the young astrophysicist or structural engineering expert: people who can move among experts from other nations to divine what secrets there might be to acquire, and the secrets that conversely have to be defended from enemies.

This is one profession where the robots can never take over: artificial intelligence will never replicate that blend of ruthlessness and personal seductiveness that any secret agent needs. Most fundamentally – as all our daydreams prove – spying is about doing transgressive things for the noblest and most moral motives. Whether it is cracking the safe, or gulling a senior quantum physicist into talking about the incredible breakthroughs they have made with nuclear fusion, it is about practising the dark skills of a master-criminal – but in the cause of the higher good.

And actually – as the recruiters of the security agencies will surely divine on a daily basis – the desire to be a spy might simply come from the fact that people crave the enduring appeal of adventure. Like Daphne Park no doubt experienced when she wandered into the heart of a KGB building and suddenly had to escape, this is the oldest addiction of all: the heavy heart-thump of pure adrenaline.

So it is to be hoped that these puzzles will have stirred your own imagination – and indeed made you wonder if it might now be time to offer your own secret services to the nation . . .

FURTHER READING

Andrew, Christopher, *The Defence of the Realm: The Authorized History of the MI5* (Allen Lane, 2009)

Hayes, Paddy, *Queen of Spies: Daphne Park* (Gerald Duckworth & Co. Ltd, 2015)

Jeffrey, Keith, *MI6: The History of the Secret Intelligence Service 1909-1949* (Bloomsbury, 2010)

Smith, Michael, *Six: The Real James Bonds* (Biteback Publishing, 2010)

ANSWERS

CHAPTER ONE

THE TAP ON THE SHOULDER

1

A FIRST ASSIGNMENT

MEMO from HEAD OF SECTION: 'Did you follow the instructions carefully or were you desperate to begin? If you did follow the instructions you would not have solved the puzzles at all. Instruction c) is crystal clear. You were instructed to "take no further action". If you did solve the puzzles, do beware. From now on follow all the instructions very carefully.'

a) In this section there are no words containing the letter 'e', one of the most widely used letters in the English language.

b) The first and last words in each of these sentences are all made from letters that are also used as Roman numerals, i.e. I, V, X, L, C, D and M.

2

BUILDING BLOCKS

The words rearranged in the correct order are: KEYHOLE, ARCHWAY, STEEPLE, CHIMNEY, TEMPLES, BOUDOIR, MANSION. The formed word is KREMLIN.

3

DIARY DATE

The words in the question can be completed by inserting the abbreviation for a month of the year in the blank spaces. Adjunct – Jun, Capricious – Apr, Dismayed – May, Doctorate – Oct, Gauged – Aug, Innovative – Nov, Indecisive – Dec, Lifeboat – Feb, Remarkable – Mar, Transept – Sept, Trojans – Jan.

One month is missing – July, so that is the month of your holiday.

4

FOR SAFE KEEPING

All the numbers on the outer ring can be made by adding two numbers from the inner ring, with the exception of just three. These are: 11, 28 and 34. If you found these then you can open the safe.

5

HYMN PRACTICE

From the pulpit, Reverend Cheetham makes this announcement: 'Move the 8 from the third column to the foot of the middle column. Move the 9 from the middle column to the foot of the right hand column, turning it over at the same time so that it reads 6. Now all the columns will add up to 18.'

6

LINKS

The links are: Dutch agent will fly here Sunday. Can hold key to code.

7

MISSING DELEGATIONS

1 BELGIAN, **2** IRISH, **3** TURKISH, **4** FRENCH,
5 HUNGARIAN, **6** ENGLISH, **7** SPANISH, **8** DANISH,
9 SWISS, **10** GREEK.

The missing countries are: SOUTH AFRICA, BRAZIL and MEXICO.

8

NEW RECRUIT

The password is PAGE. The two word squares are:

P	O	E	M
O	L	G	A
E	G	G	S
M	A	S	K

B	A	G	S
A	U	R	A
G	R	A	Y
S	A	Y	S

9

ON THE MOVE

You need a mode of transport to complete the words and this is how you will reach the locations.

1 BUS, **2** VAN, **3** CAB, **4** TRAM.

10

SHADOWY SQUARE

Uncle, Noose, Dover, Enemy, Rural. Horizontal squares reveal UNDER COVER.

11

SPY RINGS

G has most links, with four connections. A has no links. B has one link. C has one link. D has two links. E has three links. F has two links. H has one link.

12

TOUR OF DUTY

He goes from CHINA to IRAN to UKRAINE to GERMANY and ends in BULGARIA.

13

VALUED AGENTS

ANNETTE IS AGENT 25

Letter values are: A = 1, I = 2, N = 3, T = 4, E = 5.

14

WORKING IN PAIRS

1 ESCAPES, **2** EDUCATED, **3** REASSURE,
4 ICONIC, **5** INSULIN.

Rearrange ESEDREICIN and you have the mystery couple ERIC and DENISE.

CHAPTER TWO

THE SECRETS OF THE BUTTERFLIES

1

BUTTERFLIES

ARMOUR, BARRACKS, BUOYANT, CANDIDATE, CHAPLAIN, COVERAGE, EXCELLENT, HATRED, IMPACTED, LIPSTICK, MASSACRE.

The word left over is Cater, which joins up with Pillar to make the word Caterpillar.

2

GIFT BOX

Box number 4.

3

LEFT LUGGAGE

The locker number is number 127.

4

SECRET SIGN

BANJO is the response. Move the letters in INGOT back six places in the alphabet to form CHAIN. Move the letters in KNEED back in the alphabet five places to form FIZZY. Following on the pattern, move the letters in FERNS back four places in the alphabet to form BANJO.

5

PARLOUR GAME

VERDI – IDIOT – TOWED – DRESS – (UP LADDER) – SCARF – FRUIT – TOTEM – MITRE – (DOWN SNAKE) – ESSAY – YOUTH – HOTEL – LIVER – RELIC – COYPU – UNITE – EQUIP – (UP LADDER) – PIANO – OWING – GREAT – (DOWN SNAKE) – TREES – SHACK – KOALA – (UP LADDER) – ALLOW – WALTZ – ZEBRA.

6

POINTED

WEDNESDAY EVENING, SEVEN FIFTEEN. NEXT WEEKEND WE NEED TO MEET IN THE TENT NEAR THE BEND IN THE PASS. NINE TWENTY.

7

ROAD BLOCK

Twelve is the maximum. If you were looking for a hasty retreat, one is the minimum.

8

THE 39 STEPS

START AT 7. MOVE DOWN TO 3. MOVE DOWN TO 3. MOVE DOWN TO 1. MOVE UP TO 5. MOVE DOWN TO 3. MOVE UP TO 13. MOVE DOWN TO 3. MOVE DOWN TO 1. MOVE DOWN TO 39.

CHAPTER THREE

A MAN CALLED C

1

HEARD ON THE TUBE RAILWAY

The gentleman was the second lady's uncle.

2

SIR EDWYN DE TUDOR

The distance must have been sixty miles. If Sir Edwyn left at noon and rode 15 miles an hour, he would arrive at four o'clock – an hour too soon. If he rode ten miles an hour, he would arrive at six o'clock – an hour too late. But if he went twelve miles an hour, he would reach the castle of the wicked baron exactly at 5 o'clock – the time he appointed.

3

THE MILKMAID PUZZLE

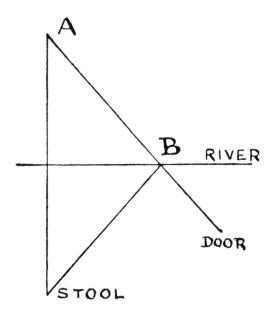

Draw a straight line, as shown in the diagram, from the milking-stool perpendicular to the near bank of the river, and continue it to the point A, which is the same distance from that bank as the stool. If you now draw the straight line from A to the door of the dairy, it will cut the river at B. Then the shortest route will be from the stool to B and thence to the door. Obviously the shortest distance from A to the door is the straight line, and as the distance from the stool to any point of the river is the same as from A to that point, the correctness of the solution will probably appeal to every reader without any acquaintance with geometry.

4

A PLANTATION PUZZLE

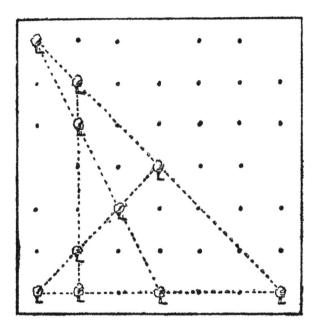

The illustration shows the ten trees that must be left to form five rows with four trees in every row. The dots represent the positions of the trees that have been cut down.

5

TURKS AND RUSSIANS

The main point is to discover the smallest possible number of Russians that there could have been. As the enemy opened fire from all directions, it is clearly necessary to find what is the smallest number of heads that could form sixteen lines with three heads in every line. Note that we say sixteen, and not thirty-two, because every line taken by a bullet may be also taken by another bullet fired in exactly the opposite direction. Now, as few as eleven points, or heads, may be arranged to form the required sixteen lines of three, but the discovery of this arrangement is a hard nut. The diagram opposite will show exactly how the thing is to be done.

If, therefore, eleven Russians were in the positions shown by the stars, and the thirty-two Turks in the positions indicated by the black dots, it will be seen, by the lines shown, that each Turk may fire exactly over the heads of three Russians. But as each bullet kills a man, it is essential that every Turk shall shoot one of his comrades and be shot by him in turn; otherwise we should have to provide extra Russians to be shot, which would be destructive of the correct solution of our problem. As the firing was simultaneous, this point presents no difficulties. The answer we thus see is that there were at least eleven Russians amongst whom there was no casualty, and that all the thirty-two Turks were shot by one another. It was not stated whether the Russians fired any shots, but it will be evident that even if they did their firing could not have been effective: for if one of their bullets killed a Turk, then we have immediately to provide another man for one of the Turkish bullets to kill; and as the Turks were known to be thirty-two in number, this would necessitate our introducing another Russian soldier and, of course, destroying the solution.

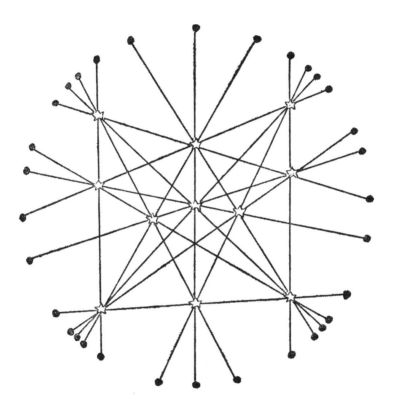

6

THE DISSECTED CIRCLE

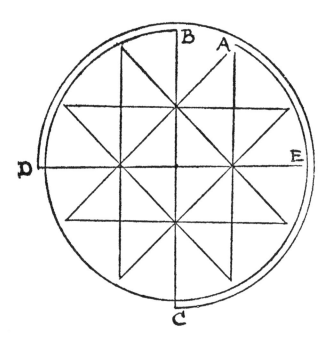

It can be done in twelve continuous strokes, thus: start downwards at A in the illustration, and eight strokes, forming the star, will bring you back to A; then one stroke round the circle to B, one stroke to C, one round to D, and one final stroke to E – twelve in all.

7

THE MONK AND THE BRIDGES

The problem of the bridges may be reduced to the simple diagram shown in the illustration. The point M represents the Monk, the point I the Island, and the point Y the Monastery. Now the only direct ways from M to I are by the bridges *a* and *b*; the only direct ways from I to Y are by the bridges *c* and *d*; and there is a direct way from M to Y by the bridge *e*. Now, what we have to do is to count all the routes that will lead from M to Y, passing over all the bridges, *a*, *b*, *c*, *d*, and *e* once and once only. With the simple diagram under the eye it is quite easy, without any elaborate rule, to count these routes methodically. Thus, starting from *a*, *b*, we find there are only two ways of completing the route; with *a*, *c*, there are only two routes; with *a*, *d*, only two routes; and so on. It will be found that there are sixteen such routes in all, as in the following list:

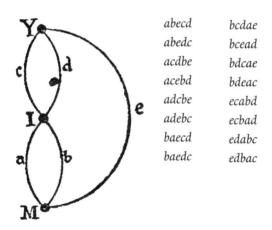

abecd	*bcdae*
abedc	*bcead*
acdbe	*bdcae*
acebd	*bdeac*
adcbe	*ecabd*
adebc	*ecbad*
baecd	*edabc*
baedc	*edbac*

223

8

THE EIGHT STARS

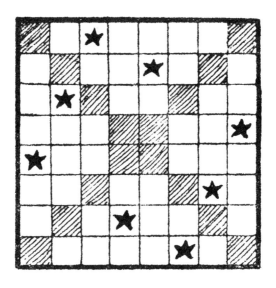

9

THE LANGUISHING MAIDEN

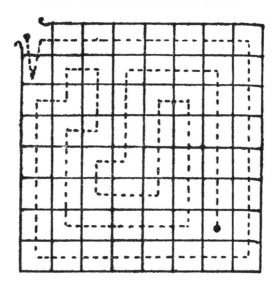

The dotted line shows the route in twenty-two straight paths by which the knight may rescue the maiden. It is necessary, after entering the first cell, immediately to return before entering another. Otherwise a solution would not be possible.

10

THE DOVETAILED BLOCK

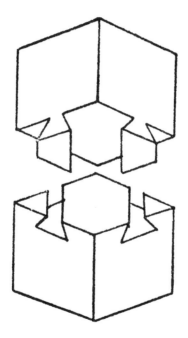

The mystery is made clear by the illustration. It will be seen at once how the two pieces slide together in a diagonal direction.

CHAPTER FOUR

LONDON CALLING

1

A LONDON LOCATION

The words are all animal anagrams:

LEOPARD, AFRICAN LION, BEARCAT

RACOON, SEAL

ZEBRA, GNU, LIONESS

You are at London Zoo.

2

DART WORDS

The message is LET HER GET THE ALE. The first score was 26, which has to be made up of a 1, 5 and 20 (he cannot use the 9 in this go so it can't be 9 + 12 + 5, the only other possibility). The corresponding letters are T, E and L, which combine to form the first word, LET. We know that the first 18 contains a single arrow score of 9. The other two numbers must be 4 and 5, giving H, E and R. The third throw does not contain a 9, so to total 18 the combination has to be 1 + 5 + 12. The letters T, E and G form the word GET. The fourth throw totals 10, which must mean he scored 1 + 4 + 5. Letters are T, H, E and THE is the only combination. The final score of 43 has to be 5 + 18 + 20. Given that you are in a pub, the only sensible combination of the letters E, A and L is the word ALE.

3

FIND THE AGENT

Each agent's name appears as three different anagrams.

1 Elgar – from regal, glare, and large.

2 Andrew – from warned, wander and warden.

3 Sadie – from ideas, aside and aides.

4 Dorset – from stored, sorted and strode.

5 Triangle – relating, integral and alerting.

4

ITMA

1 The twelve days of Christmas: 12
2 Lives of a cat: 9
3 Wonders of the ancient world: 7
4 Black squares on a chess board: 32
5 Letters in the alphabet: 26
6 Days in a leap year: 366
7 Pints in a quart: 2
8 Minutes in an hour: 60
9 Degrees in a right angle: 90
10 Degrees in a right-angled triangle: 180

The highest number is 366, the lowest is 2, so you need frequency 368.

5

GOLF, CHEESE AND CHESS

Angela likes Cheddar. Her surname is King. Her codename is Birdie.

Bill likes Edam. His surname is White. His codename is Bunker.

Carol likes Wensleydale. Her surname is Black. Her codename is Iron.

Dawn likes Stilton. Her surname is Bishop. Her codename is Eagle.

Edward likes Camembert. His surname is Castle. His codename is Flag.

6

LYRICAL

'Ev'ry Blitz your resistance toughening
From the Ritz to the Anchor and Crown,
Nothing ever could over ride
The pride of London Town.'

The letters in the word 'music' have been slotted in between the song words and then these letters have been divided into groups.

7

SOUNDS FAMILIAR

1 CURRANT, 2 SELL, 3 COURT, 4 WEIGHT, 5 ATE,
6 KNIGHTS, 7 CHEQUE, 8 STATIONERY, 9 BOARDER,
10 KERNEL, 11 SCENT, 12 FOUR, 13 AISLE, 14 RIGHT,
15 TWO, 16 HYMN, 17 INN, 18 KNOW, 19 THYME.

The messages when read out loud also gives:

Current cell caught.
Wait eight nights.
Check stationary border.
Colonel sent for.
I'll write to him in no time.

8

THE KING'S SPEECH

The speech reads, 'A new year is at hand. We cannot tell what it will bring. If it brings peace, how thankful we shall be. If it brings continued struggle, we shall remain undaunted.'

This is a substitution code. The clue was in the King always comes first. The letters REX (king) have been moved to the beginning of the alphabet and the remaining letters follow in their usual sequence. So, in the coded message the R stands for a letter A, E for a B and X for a C. In code, A is now the fourth letter of the alphabet and represents a D and the next letter, B, represents an E, and so on. Y and Z are the only letters that do not change.

CHAPTER FIVE

THE BRAIN DRAINERS

1
CAFÉ SOCIETY

There are options as to which roads to go down, but the number of changes of direction remains as follows: Tuesday is SEVEN changes of direction and on Wednesday is THIRTEEN changes of direction.

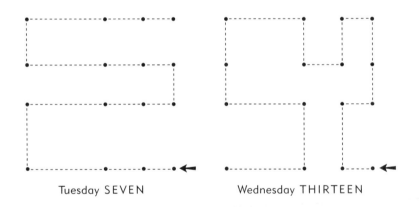

Tuesday SEVEN   Wednesday THIRTEEN

2

LYING LOW

The key words are ACT NOW.

The first grid reads as follows:
Across: ACT, SHE, HINT, DOE, ERA.
Down: ASH, CHIDE, TENOR, TEA.

The second grid reads:
Across: NOW, AWE, GNAW, EVE, RED.
Down: NAG, OWNER, WEAVE, WED.

3

MINDGAMES

The groups are as follows:

BRANDENBURG	GOLDEN	KISSING	MENIN	(famous gates)
BALL	BREAK	CUE	POCKET	(all snooker terms)
CROCUS	ROSE	SAFFRON	VIOLA	(all flowers)
BRASS	PITCH	SCORE	STRINGS	(musical terms)
LOVE	NET	RACKET	SERVE	(tennis terms)
BOX	PIT	SET	WINGS	(all found in a theatre)

4

PLAYING FOR TIME

The answer is twenty-five past eight. Our eagle-eyed counter-espionage expert has worked out that if you transfer the timings to a traditional clockface, the nearest numbers to each hand add up to thirteen. So Monday is 12 + 1. Tuesday: 9 + 4. Wednesday: 10 + 3. Thursday: 11 + 2. Friday: 9 + 4.

Therefore the final meeting is twenty-five past eight, or 8 + 5.

5

SECRET SERVICE

The London journey ends in Berlin. The Moscow journey ends in Zagreb.

C = Clockwise. A = Anticlockwise.

First journey: 1C London, 2A Lisbon, 3C Israel, 4A Prague,
                   5C Aleppo, 6A Poland, 7C Manila, 8C Madras,
                   9C Athens, 10A Bremen, 11A Berlin.

Second journey: 11A Moscow, 10C Ostend, 9A Sweden,
                   8C Dieppe, 7A Vienna, 6C Verona, 5C Lahore,
                   4A Tahiti, 3C Kuwait, 2A Galway, 1A Zagreb.

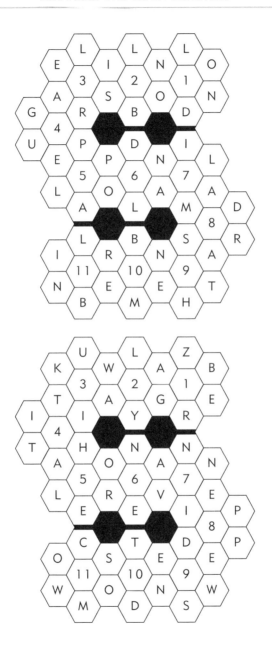

6

RENDEZVOUS

1) Four stops is the minimum. They meet at East Way.

2) The answer is Archgate. Alicia travels to Cold Lane (two stops). She then has a choice. She can take the Inner Line (two stops) and change at East Way taking the City Line (three stops) to Archgate. Alternatively, she can stay on the train to New Fields (two stops), move on to the Southern Line (one stop) changing at East Way and taking the Inner Line to City Road (one stop) before taking a City Line train to Archgate (one stop).

Boris travels to Cold Lane (two stops), then takes an Inner City train to East Way (two stops), he changes on to the City Line and travels to Archgate (three stops).

Katarina takes the Link Line to Downtown (one stop), she then gets an Inner Line train to Upper Gate (one stop) before changing on to the Southern Line and travelling to East Way (three stops). After that she travels on the Inner Line to City Road (one stop) before changing on the City Line (one stop) to reach Archgate.

Dietrich can reach Archgate by three different routes. He can go to Upper Gate (one stop), change on to the Inner Line and travel to Tower Road (four stops), before taking the City Line to Archgate (two stops). He can also go to East Way on the Southern (four stops), and change to the City Line (three stops). Or a journey to West Point, via South Station (four stops in all) gives him a change to City Line (three stops).

7

SHIPS THAT PASS . . .

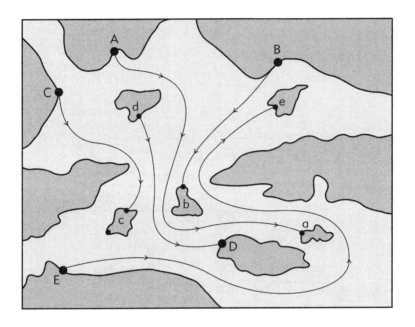

8

WOULD I LIE TO YOU?

Charles is the spy. If Andrew was the mole, then Charles and Daisy would both be telling the truth. If Brenda was guilty, then she would be lying but all the others would be telling the truth. If Daisy was guilty, then Andrew would be lying and both Charles and Daisy would be telling the truth.

With Charles the spy, he is lying along with Andrew and Brenda. Daisy is the one person telling the truth.

CHAPTER SIX

DOUBLE AGENTS? (SIX DOWN, TWO LETTERS)

1

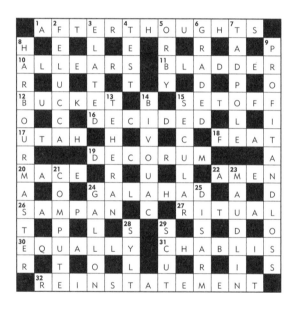

2

```
 U  P  T  O  T  H  E  M  A  R  K  ■  A  ■  I
 ■  I  M  ■  O  ■  O  ■  E  S  S  E  N  ■  N
 M  E  L  A  N  C  H  O  L  I  A  ■  S  ■  C
 ■  C  ■  H  ■  K  ■  S  ■  ■  T  R  I  G  O
 C  E  D  A  R  ■  W  E  L  L  S  ■  D  ■  H
 O  ■  A  ■  A  L  E  ■  ■  E  ■  M  U  S  E
 M  ■  Y  ■  L  ■  S  Y  N  O  D  ■  O  ■  R
 P  E  D  A  L  ■  E  ■  A  ■  I  N  U  S  E
 O  ■  R  ■  Y  P  R  E  S  ■  V  ■  S  ■  N
 S  E  E  S  ■  L  ■  T  H  E  ■  L  ■  ■  C
 ■  I  ■  A  ■  N  A  V  V  Y  S  T  Y  L  E
 T  E  M  P  O  ■  ■  E  ■  D  ■  R  ■  A  ■
 ■  I  ■  I  T  H  E  R  E  A  B  O  U  T  S
 O  U  N  C  E  ■  ■  G  ■  G  ■  U  ■  E  ■
 N  ■  G  ■  D  O  N  E  T  O  A  T  U  R  N
```

3

```
 W  E  L  L  D  O  N  E  ■  S  T  A  F  F  S
 I  ■  E  ■  A  ■  E  ■  ■  ■  O  ■  ■  ■  I
 N  O  T  K  N  O  W  N  ■  C  O  M  M  O  N
 N  ■  T  ■  G  ■  A  ■  ■  ■  ■  ■  ■  ■  G
 O  V  E  R  L  O  R  D  ■  C  H  I  L  L  S
 W  ■  R  ■  E  ■  K  E  Y  ■  O  ■  ■  ■  O
 ■  ■  ■  ■  ■  B  ■  ■  ■  O  R  D  A  I  N
 H  ■  E  S  E  R  V  A  N  T  ■  ■  R  ■  G
 A  D  V  I  C  E  ■  ■  I  ■  E  ■  ■  ■  ■
 N  ■  E  ■  ■  A  S  P  ■  ■  O  ■  S  ■  B
 D  E  N  O  T  E  ■  H  A  L  F  T  I  M  E
 I  ■  K  ■  F  ■  ■  ■  R  ■  F  ■  M  ■  G
 C  H  E  R  R  Y  ■  T  R  A  I  N  I  N  G
 A  ■  E  ■  E  ■  ■  ■  T  ■  O  ■  C  ■  E
 P  A  L  L  E  T  ■  O  T  H  E  R  E  N  D
```

4

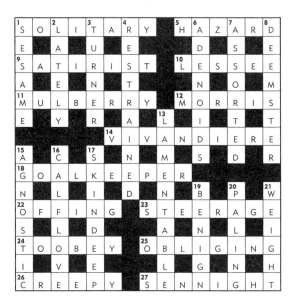

5

CHAPTER SEVEN

DEADLIER THAN THE MALE

1

A SERIES OF TYPING ERRORS

The errors are not errors at all. One word in each sentence needs to have a single letter changed. Grind becomes grand, hovel becomes hotel, ovens becomes opens, dairy becomes daily, untie becomes until and match becomes march. When you have done this the words in order form a message, reading: Grand Hotel opens daily until March.

2

CROSS PURPOSES

1 DANUBE, 2 AFRICA, 3 PEACOCK, 4 HOLLAND, 5 NAPLES, 6 EQUATOR, 7 PRAGUE, 8 AUSTRIA, 9 RUSSIA, 10 KARACHI.

The coded letters spell out: QUEEN OF SPIES, a biography of the famous Daphne Park.

3

COFFEE SHOP

Your contact is Alice who is fourth in the queue with a Latte and a croissant. In first place is Mollie with an Americano and a cupcake. Behind her is Camilla with a Mocha and a flapjack, while in third place Lizzie is about to enjoy a Cappuccino with a muffin.

4

DEAR PAM

Dear Pam is an anagram of 'read map'. The first letter of each line of the poem spells out 'Theatre at noon.'

5

KEEPING WATCH

Ms Birch has allotment D and grows vegetables. She spends 14 hours per week on her allotment.

Mrs Forrest grows fruit on allotment C, spending 9 hours a week doing so.

Mr Hedges spends 12 hours a week growing herbs on allotment A.

Mrs Lawn, from allotment B, grows alpines for 7 hours per week.

Mr Woods grows shrubs on plot E for 18 hours per week.

The two gardeners to keep a particular watch on are Mrs Forrest and Mrs Lawn.

6

LIBRARY SECRETS

The books where the secrets are hidden are ON A WHIM and VOW TO MARY. The other titles are made up of letters which are totally symmetrical, A, H, I, M, O, T, U, V, W, X, Y.

7

SHADOWED

At every junction, always select the name that is nearest the beginning of the alphabet. The route is: Long Road, Back Lane, Dog Street, Lost Lane, Cow Road, Silent Street, Green Lane, Tatler Road, Crown Street, Cooper Street, Leslie Street, Arcade Lane, Lamb Lane, Box Road, Cutler Street, Olive Lane, Lever Street, Railway Road.

8

WHEELS WITHIN WHEELS

1 CIPHER, 2 AMBUSH, 3 REGIME, 4 ORDERS, 5 TREATY, 6 BANTER, 7 INCOME, 8 GUIDED, 9 HAVING, 10 MOORED, 11 OMEN, 12 ROTA, 13 QUAY, 14 IDEA, 15 ONCE, 16 COPY, 17 QUIT, 18 AUNT, 19 EDIT, 20 ARTS, 21 MEMO, 22 SEEK, 23 THEN, 24 YEAR, 25 EDGE.

The word that doesn't fit is DEBS (short for debutantes, young society ladies presented at court).

CHAPTER EIGHT

CHAPTER AND VERSE

1

THE LANGUAGE OF LIDO

The grammatical rules of Lido are as follows:

Nouns: end in -eek if they are plural
Verbs: end in -d in present tense; end in -ded in present continuous
Word order: there is no set order

GLOSSARY:

ap: on
bey: lady
cin: with
da: from
ean: three
eil: two
end: and
ent: four
eou: man
etd: like
hei: five
icti: play
illk: rabbit

iver: animal
kiddleek: children
las: chicken
lid: watch
luny: away
man: one
mon: steal
nard: run
ogge: egg
ord: eat
ric: drop
tim: fox

N.B. Because there is no set word order, there can be variations within these answers. So for example in 1 a) the answer could also be 'the men are watching the animals'.

a) i. The animals are watching the men.
      ii. The rabbit likes the man and the chicken.

b) i. Illkeek end laseek etd eoueek.
      ii. Tim lided las nard luny.

c) i. The man and the lady watch the chicken.
      ii. The men play with two rabbits.

d) i. Eou lid tim end tim lid eil laseek.
      ii. Ean illkeek eil laseek end bey nard luny.

e) i. The foxes are eating two rabbits.
      ii. The fox watches the man drop three eggs.

f) i. Beyeek lided tim mon hei oggeek.
      ii. Eoueek end kiddleek etd ivereek.

2

CODE POEMS

a) The double agent has flown to the Alps with case A.

b) The atomic device is in the museum and primed ABC.

c) The uranium is being smuggled in the hockey pucks ABC.

d) Enemy base is hidden below disused tube station.

CHAPTER NINE

WHOSE SIDE ARE YOU ON?

1

CROSS-SECTION

ABI, BET, ENA, EVE, HAL, PAT, SID AND VIC
are on the left.

DES, RAY, MEL, NED, TED, RON, LES AND TIM
are on the right.

The words are Abides, Betray, Enamel, Evened, Halted, Patron, Sidles and Victim.

2

DOUBLE BLUFF

ACROSS:
3 SHRUB, **5** JETTY, **8** OCCUR, **9** SOUTH, **10** SWIGS,
12 CEASE, **13** EQUAL, **14** SIEGE.

DOWN:
1 CHEER, **2** QUITS, **4** SCOWL, **5** JUDGE, **6** YOKEL,
7 STASH, **11** SQUID, **12** CARGO.

3

HUNT OUT THE MOLE

I	M	P	S
M	O	L	E
P	L	E	A
S	E	A	M

C	O	M	B
O	B	O	E
M	O	L	E
B	E	E	F

S	L	I	M
L	U	D	O
I	D	O	L
M	O	L	E

4

IN CONVERSATION

Mortimer is the outsider. He has not revealed a colour in his conversation, colour being the cryptic code the others were waiting to hear. Names of colours are spelled out as consecutive letters between adjoining words.

Barrington revealed red. Caruthers revealed orange. Grenville revealed rose. Hildebrand revealed grey. Willoughby revealed green.

5

SAFE HOUSE

The order in which you will visit the seven houses is: Juanita, Raphael, Elspeth, Olympia, Ezekiel, Tiffany, Gustave. To work out the name you need take the first letter of the name in the first house you visit, the second in the second house and so on until you reach the safe house. So the letters you pick up will be: J A S M I N E.

6

SELECTION PROCESS

The comments link either to the RIGHT or the LEFT. A: If you depend on someone you can bank on them. Artistic upbringing links to the LEFT Bank in Paris. B: A fake is a copy. Links to copyRIGHT. C: Defines someone who is gauche, which is French for LEFT. D: Links to the RIGHT honourable. E: All words can be preceded by the word OVER, which links to LEFTOVER. F: Describes a RIGHT hand man. G: A pantomime villain always enters stage LEFT. H: The word links to RIGHT. I: Means LEFT. J: Means RIGHT. Following the established pattern, Agent K will be on the LEFT side.

7

TAKE TWO

```
 ¹D  U  ²C  K  ³S  ■  ⁴B  O  ⁵A  ■  ⁶R  I  ⁷G  H  ⁸T
 I   ■  U   ■  L   ■  O   ■  C   ■  I   ■  E   ■  I
 ⁹C  O  R   D  I   A  L   ■  ¹⁰C A  B   I  N   E  T
 E   ■  R   ■  P   ■  S   ■  O   ■  S   ■  E   ■  L
 ¹¹D R  E   W  ■   ¹²S T   O  U   T  ■   ¹³F R   E  E
 ■   N  ■   ¹⁴C ■  E  ■   N  ¹⁵S ■  A   ■
 ¹⁶P I  T   C  H   E  R   ■  ¹⁷T U  M   B  L   E  ¹⁸R
 O   ■  ■   E  ■   ■  ■   ■  E   ■  ■   ■  ■   ■  O
 ¹⁹P A  ²⁰T I  E   N  ²¹T ■  ²²S W  A   L  ²³L  O  W
 ■   R  ■   K  ■   R  ■   ■  A   ■  R   ■  E   ■
 ²⁴B L  U   E  ■   ²⁵C O   A  C   H  ■   ²⁶D A   S  ²⁷H
 R   ■  M   ²⁸H ■  T  ■   K  ²⁹E ■  F   ■  I
 ³⁰E X  P   L  O   I  T   ■  ³¹I N  V   A  L   I  D
 A   ■  E   ■  P   ■  E   ■  N   ■  E   ■  E   ■  E
 ³²K I  T   E  S   ■  ³³R A  G   ■  ³⁴N O   T  E   S
```

8

THE THIRD MAN

1 TOM, **2** IAN, **3** NAT, **4** KIT, **5** ALF.

CHAPTER TEN

THE MINISTRY OF SCALLYWAGS

1

BIRD'S-EYE VIEW

The square is 13.

2

CAREFUL CONCEALMENT

1 HELMET, **2** GLOVES, **3** CARDIGAN,
4 PULLOVER, **5** RAINCOAT.

3

DISGUISED

1 STUDENT, **2** BOREDOM, **3** GUNSHOT, **4** HECTARE,
5 MOORHEN, **6** DEPOSIT, **7** PLAYERS.

The hidden word is: DESTROY.

4

FOOD FOR THOUGHT

L	A	W	S		F		V	I	E	W
U		A	C	R	O	B	A	T		A
T	U	N	A		X		G	E	A	R
E	N	T	R	Y		B	U	M	P	Y
	K		F	A	B	L	E		P	
K	E	Y		C		I		F	L	Y
	M		C	H	E	S	T		A	
S	P	R	A	T		S	H	R	U	B
E	T	O	N		J		R	O	D	E
N		P	A	R	A	S	O	L		A
D	U	E	L		R		W	E	A	K

ACROSS: 1 Laws, 5 View, 8 Acrobat, 9 Tuna, 11 Gear, 13 Entry, 15 Bumpy, 16 Fable, 17 Key, 18 Fly, 19 Chest, 21 Sprat, 23 Shrub, 26 Eton, 28 Rode, 29 Parasol, 30 Duel, 31 Weak.

DOWN: 1 Lute, 2 Want, 3 Scarf, 4 Fox, 5 Vague, 6 Item, 7 Wary, 10 Unkempt, 12 Applaud, 14 Yacht, 15 Bliss, 19 Canal, 20 Throw, 21 Send, 22 Rope, 24 Role, 25 Beak, 27 Jar.

The twenty-five unused letters spell out: 'Soak this paper and eat at once'. This instruction is taken from a Special Operations guide from World War II, which describes paper that disintegrates in water and can then be eaten to destroy the evidence. The guide says it has a 'disagreeable taste' so don't try this at home!

5

ON TRACK

It takes a few moves, but it can be done. Directions are abbreviated to N, S, E and W. The engine drives N into the loop of track, then backs up heading S. The engine picks up coach 2, pulls it W then reverses it to the exit siding. The uncoupled engine goes back on to the loop of track and travels S, then on across the area E of the track with the weight restriction. At N the engine couples with coach 1 and pushes it into the exit siding. Coach 1 and 2 are coupled, with 2 nearest to the locked gates. The engine then pulls them both on to the track between W and N. The engine then reverses to push both 1 and 2 on to the S side of the track. 1 and 2 are uncoupled. The engine pulls 1 to the far W side of the track, then reverses and pushes 1 into the exit siding and leaves it there. The engine goes back to pick up coach 2, pulls it to the far N portion of the track and leaves it there. The engine moves E, S, W and returns to the exit siding. Coach 1 is then coupled to the engine and is pulled from the siding on to the track loop W. The engine reverses S. Coach 1 is uncoupled and left where coach 2 first stood. The engine heads W, before reversing in to its original position in the exit siding.

6

SOMETHING TO HIDE

1 C: CHILL, CHOP, COAT, CRESTED, **2** A: AGAIN, AGENT,
AHEAD, AMAZE, **3** I: ICONIC, IRATE, IRON, IVAN,
4 T: THATCH, TRAIN, TROUBLE, TWIGS **5** H: HEATING,
HEDGES, HERRING, HOWL, **6** N: NAILED, NARROW, NEAR,
NICE, **7** I: IDEAL, ION, IRAN, IRISES.

The letters C, A, I, T, H, N, and I can be rearranged to spell out
CHIANTI.

7

SPECIAL DELIVERY

The top-secret consignments are each being delivered by five different modes of transport hidden in the apparently random messages.

1 CAR, **2** SKIFF, **3** PUNT, **4** TRAIN, **5** CYCLE.

8

TINNED FOODS

1 BROTH/MINCE, **2** MANGO/PEACH, **3** KIPPER/SALMON,
4 CHERRY/DAMSON, **5** ANCHOVY/SARDINE.

CHAPTER ELEVEN

THE THRILLING DENOUEMENT

1

BEAT THE CLOCK

The device needs to be turned anticlockwise. Fifteen words are entered anticlockwise (A) and thirteen words are written clockwise (C).

1 PASSPORT (A), **2** AIRFIELD (C), **3** RECKLESS (A),
4 COMMANDO (C), **5** EVIDENCE (A), **6** HANDCUFF (C),
7 SKIRMISH (C), **8** AMBUSHED (A), **9** BEFRIEND (C),
10 OVERHEAR (C), **11** FUGITIVE (C), **12** APPROACH (C),
13 DISGUISE (A), **14** DIRECTOR (C), **15** CROSSING (A),
16 STRANGER (C), **17** SABOTAGE (C), **18** ASSASSIN (C),
19 TIME BOMB (A), **20** TRAINING (A), **21** COLLECTS (A),
22 STILETTO (C), **23** DIPLOMAT (A), **24** BETRAYAL (A),
25 SCHEDULE (A), **26** TRANSMIT (A), **27** IMPOSTOR (A),
28 QUESTION (A).

2

DIGITAL DEVICES

Key the numbers into a traditional calculator, turn upside down to reveal the messages.

1 SOS ELLIE IS ILL. **2** LEE SEES SOIL. **3** HOLLIE SELLS SHOES. **4** SHE IS LOIS HILL. **5** ELSIE LOSES LESS.

3

DIPLOMACY

F	CH	I	D	NL	GB	B	L	E
E	L	D	B	F	CH	NL	I	GB
GB	NL	B	L	E	I	F	D	CH
CH	E	F	NL	D	B	L	GB	I
D	B	NL	GB	I	L	E	CH	F
L	I	GB	F	CH	E	D	B	NL
I	D	CH	E	B	NL	GB	F	L
NL	F	L	CH	GB	D	I	E	B
B	GB	E	I	L	F	CH	NL	D

4

COUNTDOWN

1   1,095 (not a leap year in sight!).

2   61.

3   160. The monarchs in the first half of the twentieth century were Victoria, Edward VII, George V, Edward VIII and George VI.

The monarchs in the second half of the twentieth century were George VI and Elizabeth II. 5 x 2 x 16 = 160.

4   The 120 half crowns are worth £15. The 144 10p pieces are worth £14.40.

5   There are 604,800 seconds in a week and 528,000 feet in 100 miles.

5

ELIZABETHAN ESPIONAGE

	♩	𝅗𝅥	𝅝	♩	♪
𝄞	A	J	K	T	U
♯	B	I	L	S	V
♭	C	H	M	R	W
𝄢	D	G	N	Q	X
⌒	E	F	O	P	YZ

The illustration shows the order in which the letters of the alphabet fit into the grid and provides the solution to the code. Message reads: 'Help. Rebels plotting. Queen in grave danger.'

6

EXPLOSIVE ELEMENTS

1 FUN D RUM, **2** ARE A FAR, **3** LAW N EON, **4** FAN G OAT,
5 WOK E CRU, **6** SPA R ACE, **7** TOW N EAT, **8** BID E SPY
9 ARE A BUT, **10** EWE R USE, **11** HER B RAT, **12** ALL Y OUR.

Message reads: 'Danger nearby.'

7

FLAT NUMBER

The flat is number 65. For the first sum to work, A = 9, E = 4, R =
5. The sum now reads: 459 + 495 = 954. The second sum informs
you that the three letters will equal the flat number: 9 + 4 x 5 = 65.

8

I-SPY

S	P	Y		Y	E	S
A		E	Y	E		A
T	O	W		T	I	P
	A				L	
E	R	R		S	L	Y
A		U	S	E		E
T	A	G		W	I	N

9

IMPOSTORS

The impostors are:

1 a) and c)
2 b) and c)
3 a) and b)
4 b) and c)
5 a) and c)
6 No impostors here. All definitions are correct.

10

MOVING ON

You will be moving on in a LINER and a PLANE.

MAJOR / MANOR / MINOR / MINER / LINER / LINEN.
SLANT / PLANT / PLANE / PLACE / PEACE /PENCE.

11

OUT OF ORDER

1 ALL STATIONS BE PREPARED FOR ACTION.
2 THE YOUNG MAN HAS CROSSED THE BORDER IN
DISGUISE. 3 KEEP A LOOKOUT FOR GUARD DOGS.
THEY ARE DANGEROUS.

12

VENETIAN VENTURE

The tile is second in from the right on the top line. It shows a star inside a circle. Each tile contains two shapes. The inner shape always becomes the outer shape on the following tile. The sequence repeats itself from the lowest row to the top.

ACKNOWLEDGEMENTS

First of all, with huge gratitude to Grace Paul at Headline Publishing, whose unsung ability to construct and decipher cryptic languages, while facing the remorseless countdowns of publishing deadlines, surely makes her eligible for Her Majesty's Secret Service. In the same spy vein, brilliantly presiding over a Q-Branch boffin laboratory of dazzling and devious puzzle invention are Roy and Sue Preston. Countless thanks also to Lindsay Davies, whose golden laser beam eye for editing has come to the rescue many times. Providing valuable leads and inside intelligence has been my fantastic literary agent, Anna Power. And the whole mission was conceived by departmental supremo Sarah Emsley (with emphasis on the 'eM'. . .).

If you enjoyed *Secret Agent Brainteasers*, flex your
brain further with *Bletchley Park Brainteasers*.

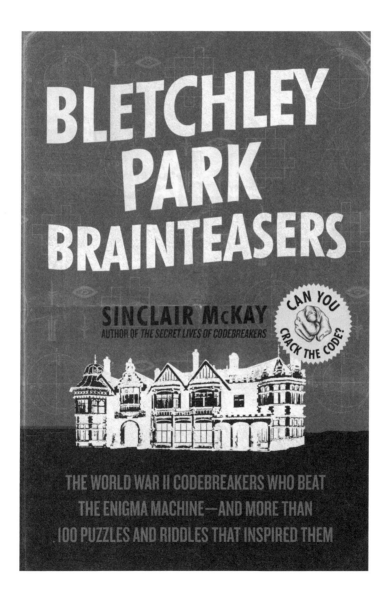

BLETCHLEY
PARK
BRAINTEASERS

SINCLAIR McKAY
AUTHOR OF *THE SECRET LIVES OF CODEBREAKERS*

CAN YOU
CRACK THE CODE?

THE WORLD WAR II CODEBREAKERS WHO BEAT
THE ENIGMA MACHINE—AND MORE THAN
100 PUZZLES AND RIDDLES THAT INSPIRED THEM